At a time when the RULES are changing, the LAWS remain constant.

You CAN change the rules.

You CANNOT break the laws.

JEFFREY GITOMER

Jeffrey GITOMER'S

21.5

UNBREAKABLE
LAWS 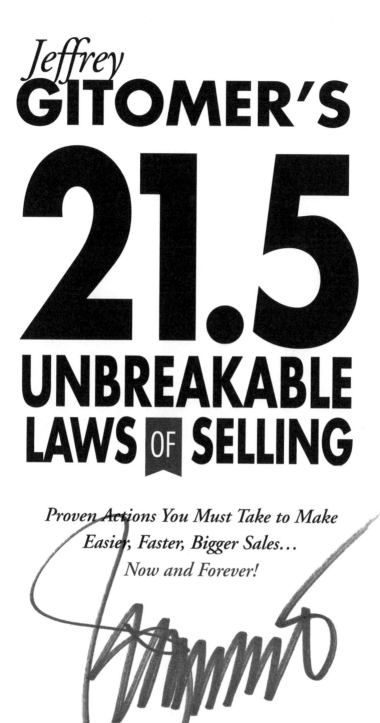 OF SELLING

Proven Actions You Must Take to Make
Easier, Faster, Bigger Sales…
Now and Forever!

Bard Press

Austin, Texas

Jeffrey Gitomer's 21.5 Unbreakable Laws of Selling: Proven Actions You Must Take to Make Easier, Faster, Bigger Sales Now and Forever

Published by Bard Press, Austin, Texas

To order additional copies of this book, contact your favorite bookseller or call Jeffrey's friendly office at 704/333-1112.

The author may be contacted at the following address:

Buy Gitomer
310 Arlington Ave, Loft 329
Charlotte, NC 28203
USA
Phone: 704/333-1112 Fax: 704/333-1011
Email: salesman@gitomer.com
Website: www.gitomer.com

ISBN-10: 1-885167-79-2
ISBN-13: 978-1-885167-79-8

Library of Congress Cataloging-in-Publication Data:

Gitomer, Jeffrey H.
  21.5 unbreakable laws of selling : proven actions you must take to make easier, faster, bigger sales... now and forever! / by Jeffrey Gitomer.
     pages cm
  ISBN 978-1-885167-79-8 -- ISBN 1-885167-79-2
  1. Selling. I. Title.
  HF5438.25.G577 2013
  658.85--dc23
                                                            2013022213

A Bard Press Book
Credits
Editor-In-Chief: Jessica McDougall
Executive Editor: Stephanie Melish
Copyeditor/Proofreader: Deborah Costenbader
Jacket Designer: Andy Horner
Typesetting/Production: Michael Wolff

Printed in the United States by RR Donnelley

First Printing, July 2013

You Don't Have to Play by the Rules to Win at Sales, but You Do Have to Follow and Implement the Laws.

Every salesperson is looking for ways to *make more sales*. Sometimes you're pressured to do so because of a quota or sales plan – and sometimes you're on a roll and just want to add to your success.

Fortunately for you there is no "one way" to make more sales happen.

REALITY: You get into selling situations where you lose the sale. You're certain that you should have won the sale but something, one thing, went wrong.

You might blame price, purchasing, bidding, the competition, or some other circumstance, but the fact is – you lost it because you broke one of the laws of selling.

Was it value versus price?
Was it your presentation skills?
Was it lack of proof?
Was it that you couldn't build trust?

Whatever it was, the result was a lost sale.

TURN BACK TIME: In the mid 1970s, I fought against fierce competitors in the heart of New York City. And I won. Ethically.

I came to realize later in life that much of my early success was based on my ability to communicate. The competition didn't have my passion or my belief – and they didn't have the ability to transfer that passion and belief to the customer.

Please don't think I made every sale I tried for. Not even close. But I can say every time I failed, I learned, and I wrote about it.

Within a few years, I began teaching others my sales ideas and strategies. I realized I was able to transfer my passion for sales in a way that others loved. They tried my suggestions and succeeded. Soon more people wanted to learn more and more of my thinking.

My evolving realization and vision became clear once I fully understood that love was at the root of my passions:

- **Once I realized I loved sales, I wanted to be the best at it.**

- **Once I realized I loved writing about sales, I wanted to be the best at it.**

- **Once I realized I loved speaking about sales, I wanted to be the best at it.**

Can you say the same about your love of what you do?

It takes time.

1. **My first ten years in sales taught me the rules of selling.**

2. **My second ten years in sales reinforced my love of selling and my belief in what I was selling.**

3. **My third ten years in sales left me with an urgency to write and speak about what I had learned so that others could use those lessons for themselves – and turn my skills and my success into their skills, their success, and their money. Better stated: your money.**

3.5 **Now, after forty years in sales, I have come to the realization there are *Unbreakable Laws* you have to follow in order to achieve the desired outcome – the sale!**

I have documented my sales knowledge and success into 21.5 Unbreakable Laws of Selling that are not just self-evident truths – they are also the foundation by which you can grow your sales success.

Once you read, understand, and begin to apply the laws of selling, you'll further understand why they cannot be broken. And once you begin to master the laws, you will be building a concrete foundation for sales and career success.

One that you have worked hard for. One that you deserve.

If you learn the laws – if you work hard to master the laws – then making sales will become easier and faster.

JEFFREY GITOMER

21.5 Unbreakable Laws of Selling
Proven Actions You Must Take to Make
Easier, Faster, Bigger Sales...
NOW and FOREVER!

Table of Contents

"When you master the laws, you will reap their rewards."
Jeffrey Gitomer

1

ATTRACT WILLING BUYERS

CHALLENGE

Does your phone ring with people who want to buy? Or (like a fool) do you still cold call? Just asking. What is the perception of your value in your marketplace? That's where I want you to dominate. Enough value, put out consistently over time, means your phone will ring – with customers who want to buy. This is the killer law.

The 95/95 Proposition.
Which 95 Are You?

When a prospective customer calls you on the phone, and for some reason or another wants to buy – either they heard something good about you, or they read something about you, or they read something you wrote, or someone referred them to you – the odds are close to 95% in your favor that you can make a sale and build a relationship.

Not bad odds.

REASON: The prospective customer called you, seeking information in the hope of making a purchase.

BACK TO REALITY: You come into your office and you sit at your desk. Today's the day you're going to (have to) make 100 phone calls (cold calls) to prospective customers.

The odds are 95% of them will end up somewhere between "no" and hang up. Bad odds. And, of the other 5% that displayed some form of interest, one *may* eventually end up buying.

The problem is you will have to go through every sales gyration and your entire sales cycle to make that happen. Product offering, appointment, proposals, biddings, follow-up ad nauseam, finding the right decision maker, and other walls of selling that you have erected based on your (or your company's) inability to be a marketplace value provider.

RECAP: You will make the sale 95% of the time when you RECEIVE an unsolicited call from a prospective customer. You will lose the sale 95% of the time when you MAKE an unsolicited call to a prospective customer.

YESTERDAY: For the past ten years (*yesterday*), it's likely that your business has been winning sales by capturing low-hanging fruit and you, as a salesperson, have thought to yourself, "I'm pretty good. I made president's club."

TODAY: All of a sudden you get to *today*, and you're looking around for fruit. It's nowhere to be found.

And now you're in scramble mode for several reasons:

1. You've built no social media platform.

2. You have no video testimonials to prove your value or the value of purchasing your product.

3. You have built little or no reputation in your marketplace.

4. Your product or your service is highly competitive, and it's difficult for you to differentiate yourself from the people you hate. Your competition.

4.5 You have no value message that you send to your existing customers week after week.

If you even have marketing messages or sales messages, they PUSH rather than PULL. They repel rather than attract.

TOMORROW: Which brings me to tomorrow. Or as they say at Disneyland, "Tomorrowland." You believe in your heart when the present economic situation changes, in "Tomorrowland" it will be way, way better, and everything will be just fine – and, of course, you will live happily ever after, making president's club again.

You might want to take that strategy next door to "Fantasyland" and shake hands with Mickey, Minnie, and especially Goofy.

There's an old expression that says, "If you want things to get better, *you* have to get better." If you haven't prepared for this time, or tomorrow, then NOW is the time to dig in. Stronger, faster, harder, and with more determination than ever.

When sales are tough, your competitors will be coming at your existing customers with offers that appeal to their pocketbook.

You have to provide valuable service, you have to be a value partner, and you have to be a value provider. If not, you'll either lose the account, or worse, be asked to match the price. (In the land of profit, matching a price is the same as losing.)

Now is the time to invest in yourself. And now is the time to invest in your customers in order to get the 95% pendulum to swing in your direction. Now is the time for value.

There are very few alternatives to what I'm recommending – and of those alternatives none are as valid as what I'm suggesting.

Many salespeople at this moment are somewhere between whiny and panicky. They're worried about their jobs when they should be worried about their customer well-being. They're worrying about the state of the world when they should be concentrating on the state of their customer loyalty.

The 95% success strategy is very simple, but it requires WORK if you want to be on the receiving end of an unsolicited call:

- **Become a consistent value provider, especially to existing customers.**

- **Use your social media platform to broadcast value messages that existing and potential customers can benefit from.**

- **Build your reputation impeccably.**

- **Get your existing customers to endorse you, support you, and stay loyal to you.**

- **Utilize the strategy employed by every great athlete:** *self-talk equals self-performance.* Tell yourself you're going to get the ball over the plate. Tell yourself you're going to hit a home run. Tell yourself you're going to return the punt for a touchdown. And picture yourself doing it.

Figure out where your value message is with respect to your customer perception of it and their willingness to receive it.

Then do the one thing that 95% of salespeople will not do: work your ass off. Today.

Free Git✗Bit...If you want a few strategies to get your phone to ring with prospective customers, go to www.gitomer.com and enter the word UNSOLICITED in the GitBit box.

In my years of achievement, hard work has always been my secret weapon. Make it yours.

JEFFREY GITOMER

Replacing the Cold Call
with: ANYTHING!

I am sick of the argument that cold calling still has a valuable place in selling. Someone PLEASE show me the value.

Let's look at the stats and the facts...

- **95% or more rejection rate**

- **100% interruption of the prospect**

- **100% they already know what you're selling**

- **100% they already have what you're selling**

- **100% manipulation to get through to the decision maker**

- **100% lack of personal preparation about the customer**

- **Most sales managers could NOT do what they ask their salespeople to do**

- **Rejection is the biggest cause of sales personnel turnover**

- **Ask any salesperson if they'd rather have 100 cold calls or ONE referral**

QUESTION: With these horrid stats, why do sales managers still insist on, even measure, cold call activity and numbers?
ANSWER: I have no earthly idea.

Cold calls suck.

Here are 12.5 real-world connection strategies to eliminate cold calling:

1. Build relationships and earn referrals. Visit existing customers. Offer ideas and help.

2. Use LinkedIn to make new connections. Use the "keyword" search feature to uncover prospects you never knew existed. Then connect without using the standard LinkedIn wording. Be original.

3. Ask your informal network of connections to recommend customers. Building and maintaining local and industry-specific relationships are critical to building your success. Pinpoint people who respect and admire your ability the same way you respect and admire theirs.

4. Network face-to-face at the highest level possible. Not an "after hours" cocktail party. Join high-level executive groups and get involved.

5. Join a business association – not a leads club. Get involved with an organization where owners gather.

6. Speak in public. All civic groups are eager to get a speaker for their weekly meeting. Be the speaker. If you give a value talk, a memorable talk, EVERY member of the audience will want to connect. You'll have the potential to gain fifty connections each time you speak.

7. Speak at trade shows. Why not get praise for the great speech you gave at the conference every time someone walks by your booth, instead of trying to get them to putt a ball into a plastic cup?

8. Write an article. Nothing breeds attraction like the written word. I am a living example of what writing can do to change a career. Become known as an expert and put yourself in front of people who can say yes to you.

9. Write an industry white paper. CEOs want to create great reputations, keep customers loyal, keep employees loyal, have no problems, maintain safety, and make a profit. Write about how your industry does that and EVERYONE will want to read it (and meet with you). White paper or brochure? You tell me... Which one gets you invited in the door? Which one earns you respect? Which one builds your reputation? And the ouch question: Which one are you using?

10. Give referrals. Yes, GIVE referrals. What better way to gain respect, cosmic indebtedness, word-of-mouth advertising, and reputation? **WARNING:** This requires hard work!

11. Send a once-a-week, value-based message to existing and prospective customers. For over a decade, my weekly article and my email magazine *Sales Caffeine* have been a major source of value to my customers and revenue to me. What's yours?

12. Contact current customers who aren't using 100% of your product line. You have gold in your own backyard. No cold call needed. Call existing customers and get more of their business.

12.5 Reconnect with lost customers. This little used strategy will net you more results than any cold call campaign on the planet. It takes courage to connect, but once you discover "why" you lost them, you can create strategies to recover the account – often more than 50% of the time.

COLD CALL TIME CHALLENGE: What is your REAL use of time making futile cold calls? That's a number you do not want to see. And how much of your use of time is a waste of time? You don't wanna see this number either.

Gotta make cold calls? Boss making you cold call? Here's the strategy for making a transition: ALLOCATE YOUR TIME.

If you have to make fifty cold calls a week, allocate enough time to connect with fifty existing or lost customers in the same week.

Then ask your boss to do both WITH YOU. Let him or her see the futility of making cold calls. Ask them to make fifty cold calls.

My bet is they can't or won't.

REALITY: You can double your sales numbers using the strategies above to attract willing buyers and your boss won't care ONE LICK if you ever make another cold call. In fact, he'll be asking you HOW YOU DID IT.

IF YOU BREAK THE LAW: You're breaking the law if you're still cold calling and prospecting. How can you possibly believe you can build a business based on long-term relationships and customer loyalty doing cold calls?

Oh, there are some companies who have been very successful making cold calls, begging for referrals, and pushing long-term untenable contracts. The penalty they pay is high turnover of customers, high turnover of sales team, and almost zero customer loyalty.

If you're breaking this law, you're struggling with numbers, bidding, proposals, price, and assorted other barriers that significantly lower the percentage of your ability to make a sale, let alone earn a sale.

IF YOU FOLLOW THE LAW: When you attract willing buyers, your phone will ring with people ready to make a purchase. Your job is to take yes for an answer – and be friendly, helpful, and easy to do business with.

There are many other benefits that go along with your phone ringing:

- It reinforces your philosophy of doing business.

- Your self-belief, self-confidence, and self-pride are through the roof.

- You don't have to "qualify buyers" – they're qualified by virtue of the fact they called you.

- All you have to do is HELP them.

- Price fights are no longer an issue.

- Morale is up.

- And so are sales!

CAUTION: This law makes too much sense. That's the easy part. This law takes work. That's the hard part.

Don't be like most salespeople who are unwilling to do the hard work it takes to make selling easy.

AHA! Cold calling is dead. The only people who don't know it are the people still doing it.

Would you rather have one referral or 100 cold calls?

AHA! Invest your time in what will give you the greatest return.

KEY TO IMPLEMENTATION: "Winning 95%" is a process, not just a strategy. This concept will take time to implement. That's the good news. It will keep all the "gotta make my goal this month or die" people and companies away. And no, this is not a "Google ad word" process. This is what is known as a long-term strategy, with long-term impact.

Yes, there is a ramp-up. A ramp-up that's dependent upon your current platform, type of messaging, immediate sales needs, and a leader with vision. That's the "process" part.

My challenge to you is that attracting willing buyers is a major key to long-term sales success, and it's ripe for the taking.

If you start today, it will take you six months to get it going, and one year to make it happen. After that, the phone will ring.

How do I know this to be true? I have been on the upside of 95% for the past twenty years.

MEASUREMENT: My personal measuring stick is Twitter. My daily goal is to be re-tweeted and favored 100 times a day.

Make it your goal to be re-tweeted ten times a day. Measure how much someone values your message by when they let THEIR entire Twitter following know it's worthwhile. That will get you on the path to the real 95%.

THINK YES!

CHALLENGE

How is your attitude? Or should I ask, how is the *consistency* of your attitude? Or should I ask, do you have a YES! Attitude? Or should I ask, how *transferable* is your attitude? These are questions that might make you a bit uncomfortable, but you must recognize that attitude is fundamental and foundational to sales success. If your attitude vacillates or is challenged by outside circumstances (customer rejection, changes in compensation plans, competition), it's time you harness the power of attitude for a lifetime of peace and success in sales.

What Is the Importance of Attitude?

Every person, you included, wants to achieve more, earn more, find happiness, be successful, and be fulfilled. Oh, and make more sales!

At the root of all these elements is attitude – positive attitude – your positive attitude.

Every person, you included, instinctively knows that. Yet most haven't fully embraced or discovered their positive attitude.

- **Most people don't focus on their attitude.**
- **Most people don't study attitude.**
- **Most people don't practice attitude.**
- **Most people don't live the essence of attitude.**
- **Most people don't live the principles of attitude.**
- **Most people are not dedicated to attitude.**
- **Most people have never read a book on attitude.**

You included?

I believe I was born with a positive attitude, and I believe you were born with a positive attitude. It took twenty-four years for me to discover mine. I wonder if you have found yours yet.

Here's an expression you've heard before: "Attitude is everything!"

But let me break down the elements of that expression for you – maybe for the first time. Attitude controls, rules, affects, and directs your career, your family life, your personal life, and you. It affects or can impact your relationships, your business success, and your health.

In my *Little Gold Book of YES! Attitude* I explain the difference between "positive" and "YES!" When something great happens, you don't scream "POSITIVE!" When something great happens, you scream "YES!"

It's a subtle, but powerful, difference in thinking when you come to that mental and verbal understanding.

What language do you speak? No, I don't mean Spanish, French, or English. I mean positive or negative. Attitude language.

The other day I was looking out the window at the pouring rain. "It's gonna be a rotten day," I said to my partner. "I don't think so," said Jessica, in a soft, reassuring tone. (She never lets the weather get to her. She grew up in Seattle!) She was thinking about "the day" not "the weather."

It's the wording of expressions like that, that can lead to a "bad day" for anyone. Even you. A rotten day starts with the way you think about it, and the way you talk about it. It's not about the weather outside. It's about the weather inside – inside your mind.

- **How's the weather where you live?**

- **How's the weather where you work?**

- **How's the weather where you play?**

- **How's the weather where you think?**

Positive attitude is often defined as, "The way you dedicate yourself to the way you think." You are in complete control of it.

Think YES!

Thinking positive is a self-discipline. A daily self-discipline. You control it. You make it happen. Or not.

Taking positive actions is dependent on positive thought. If you don't THINK positive, you will not BE positive, and you will not DO positive.

There are many definitions of attitude, and there are many ways to look at attitude. Books have been written on attitude that you may not have exposed yourself to. All of them contain insight that can help you. It's a matter of exposing yourself to them and then discovering what's for you and what can help you achieve your positive attitude.

Books like *How to Win Friends and Influence People*, by Dale Carnegie, or *Think & Grow Rich*, by Napoleon Hill, contain the philosophies, strategies, and the connected stories of men and women who have achieved their positive attitude – and can help you achieve yours.

You should own them and read a few pages every day. (That's one of the secrets of attitude: read and study attitude for fifteen minutes a day.)

HERE'S THE GREAT NEWS: Positive attitude is yours for the taking, all you have to do is read, study, and apply – every day.

The ultimate challenge of discovering and living with a positive attitude is for you to decide you're willing to dedicate the time, and that you have the desire, to make it happen for yourself.

Attitude is bigger than selling.

It's bigger because:

- **Your attitude permits sales to take place and relationships to blossom.**

- **Your attitude is the only known cure for continuous rejection.**

- **Your attitude is the spark that lights your personality and the driving force behind your presentation.**

And when you turn your attitude heat up high (passion and enthusiasm), you can transfer your attitude to your customer – making THEM feel great, and setting a buying atmosphere.

Free Git木Bit...If you want additional ideas for the achievement of a positive attitude, go to www.gitomer.com and enter the words ATTITUDE STARTERS in the GitBit box.

When you think YES! you will see the possibilities, not the impossibilities.

JEFFREY GITOMER

What Makes You Smile?
What Changes Your Mood?

PICTURE THIS: Just landed at JFK airport after an eight-hour flight from London. Me, Jessica, and Gabrielle, our then one-year-old daughter.

By the age of one, Gabrielle was already a seasoned flyer. Atlantic Ocean twice, Pacific Ocean three times, and on her maiden voyage to Europe she collected six stamps on her passport. She made the London to New York flight whimper-free, and now faces a three-hour layover to catch yet another flight home to Charlotte, North Carolina.

We take the AirTran from Terminal 4 to Terminal 7, and go through security again, not really looking forward to the three-hour wait.

NOTE: When you fly a lot, you can't complain about jet lag. Over the years, I have created my own philosophy about time zones: I'm in my own time zone. When I land, it's either daytime or nighttime. I make a mental adjustment to the time of day, and when I do, the physical seems to follow.

Anyway, we get to Terminal 7, hungry, and we are looking around for some tasty, overpriced food. We spot something that looks edible at one of those fresh-made sandwich places.

I go up to the counter and spy a cut-open avocado on the back counter. I get an egg salad sandwich, Jessica gets a turkey and cheddar sandwich, and I ask the woman who is serving us if we could please purchase some avocado to give to Gabrielle.

"We don't sell avocado!" she barked.

I challenged her a couple of times, and although there was an avocado cut wide open on the counter behind her, she stuck fiercely to her guns in a typical Northeast, it's my way or the highway, manner – without a smile, matter of fact, and if you don't like it, go someplace else.

She walked away.

Another woman behind the counter, who witnessed the avocado exchange and felt empathy for the baby in my arms, came over and said, "How about an avocado sandwich?" "Great!" I said, "Thank you!"

She smiled, and in a minute and a half had cut the entire avocado up, placed it between two slices of bread, and wrapped it.

I looked at the wrapper. It read, "Three cheese sandwich." The woman smiled at me and said, "We don't actually sell avocado. This will help you with the cashier."

I paid and sat down at our table. We ate our sandwiches and fed the baby. I went back to the counter to thank the woman again and handed her a $10 bill. She smiled at me, almost in tears, and said, "Thank you" as she looked me in the eye.

I love the exchange of random acts of kindness.

Meanwhile, our plane home is delayed another hour. The airport is full of people, mostly New York people, mostly New York people with an attitude that's compounded by flight delay.

Finally we board. Because we have the baby, we board first. Sitting in Row 1, Jessica immediately straps Gabrielle in her car seat, gets her DVD player rolling, and places the player between Gabrielle's legs.

Sesame Street begins to play, Gabrielle's legs are now positioned alongside the player, and she looks about as laid back as humanly possible with red headphones on, bouncing and grooving to the Sesame Street sounds of "Who are the people in your neighborhood?"

I am positioned across the aisle in seat 1D, so I can see people boarding the plane. As they're boarding, every single person is looking glum, either angry at the delay, prices in the airport, or the world.

As each passenger turns the corner to find their seat, they look at Gabrielle and immediately begin to smile. If two people are traveling together they begin to smile, point, and talk. "Look at that cute baby watching a movie!" They stop to revel in Gabrielle's joy.

For the next eleven minutes, every single person who boarded the plane stopped, smiled, pointed, and even commented to total strangers.

Gabrielle, in her innocence, and being herself, had changed the mood of the entire plane. Even the flight attendants were marveling, and people were actually taking pictures.

What mood are you in? What changes your mood? How easy is it for you to go from a good mood to bad, or bad to good?

Most people who are rarely in a good mood don't realize they have a choice. Gabrielle created a rare opportunity to change 137 moods in an instant. Everyone occasionally needs a mood change. Find yours, and employ it to trigger a better mood – even a great mood – in an instant.

IF YOU BREAK THE LAW: The attitude law is exceptionally breakable, especially if your attitude is easily tipped from positive to neutral to negative. When you break the attitude law, everyone around you is affected: your family, your friends, your coworkers, and your customers. Typically, your positive attitude is broken on a reactionary basis – your response to something that happened. The remedy is simple: think before you respond. Ask a question rather than make a statement. And most important, consider the source.

IF YOU FOLLOW THE LAW: Attitude is magic. It's both transferable and contagious. It sets the tone for meetings, communication, and your relationships. And it builds your reputation as a happy person.

It's amazing how positive attitude, YES! Attitude, can create engagement, agreement, harmony, and sales. To me, one of the most powerful aspects of attitude is your focus on why something can happen, not why it can't.

CAUTION: Attitude requires consistency. It can't be a part-time, sometime, or most of the time thing. Attitude has to be all of the time.

KEY TO IMPLEMENTATION: If you're looking for a secret, here's the one I use: I perform at least one random act of kindness a day, and I create at least ten smiles a day from people I interact with.

Try it. The results, and the smiles, will amaze you.

Attitude has power. Personal power. And the best part is: YOU CONTROL IT.

You determine the way you think about, develop, and deliver your attitude.

JEFFREY GITOMER

BELIEVE BEFORE YOU SUCCEED

CHALLENGE

If you're looking for the secret sauce of making more sales and more money, the fulcrum point is your belief system. The way you believe in your company, your product, your ability to convey your message, your ability to differentiate yourself from your competitor, your ability to prove value to your customer, and your deep belief that the customer is better off having purchased from you will lead you to more sales, and a fat wallet. The key to understanding belief is understanding the source of belief. Belief does not come from your head, belief comes from your heart. Start there.

Are You a True Believer or Just a Salesperson?

What do you believe in? What are your real beliefs?

I'm asking you these questions so you can have a clearer picture as to why sales are made or lost.

"Jeffrey, you don't understand," you whine. "Our customers are price buyers!" No Jackson, YOU don't understand. You BELIEVE they're price buyers. Until you change your belief, they will continue to be that way.

SIMPLE RULE: Change your beliefs and you can change your outcomes.

SIMPLER RULE: Your beliefs control your sales performance.

SIMPLEST RULE: You can strengthen your beliefs with clear thoughts and deep commitment.

THINK ABOUT THIS: As you're preparing for a sale, your belief system is so powerful it will dominate your desire to win. Those beliefs have been present either consciously or subconsciously for as long as you have been employed by your present company – and they deepen with every sales call you make, every sale you achieve, and every sale you lose.

You may look at belief as "faith." A common belief is, "I've lost faith in my company's ability to deliver as promised." Others are loss of faith in the product, boss, ethics of the company, or even the economy.

There are five elements to belief, and in order to be a great salesperson you must be the master believer of all five. There's also a .5 that enables you to change or strengthen your beliefs.

1. You have to believe you work for the greatest company in the world.

2. You have to believe your products and services are the greatest in the world.

3. You have to believe in yourself.

(NOTE: STOP here and do some major soul-searching. If the above three beliefs – company, products and services, and self – are not present and deep, the next 2.5 will be impossible to comprehend, let alone master...)

4. You have to believe in your ability to differentiate from your competition in a way that the customer PERCEIVES as BOTH different AND valuable. If the customer fails to perceive a difference between you and your competition, if they fail to perceive your value, then all that's left is price.

5. You must believe that the customer is BETTER OFF having purchased from you. Not just believing this in your head. Rather, believing it in your heart.

5.5 You control your belief with your thoughts and your attitude. And understanding this is critical to building and maintaining a positive belief for all you say and do. Once this belief begins to falter, it's time to go. Time to move on to something you believe in.

These 5.5 elements to belief will drive your preparation, and thereby your presentation, to new heights, new sales, and new success.

BEWARE: There are negative beliefs that can limit your success, even if you possess the critical five.

- **Belief that your prices are too high.**
- **Belief that your competition has a lock on the business you're trying to get.**
- **Belief that the sale is a bidding process, and you'll lose without the lowest bid.**
- **Belief that the sale you're in the middle of won't happen.**

GREAT NEWS: The deeper you possess the 5.5 elements of belief, the less likely the negative beliefs are to surface and the faster your sales cycle will end – with an order.

KEY POINT OF UNDERSTANDING: Belief does not come in a day – it comes day-by-day – slowly over time. But once achieved at its highest level, it's virtually impenetrable – and it will put passion in your preparation, not to mention money in your pocket.

Do you believe? I hope you do. Your sales and your success depend on it.

Your belief and your belief system are the root of your sales success, or the bane of your failure.

JEFFREY GITOMER

Here Comes Santa Claus, Here Comes Santa Claus!

In 1972, when I was studying sales, positive attitude, and self-belief, I watched a movie called "Challenge to America" almost every day.

In it was a story told by the great Glenn W. Turner where he wrote a letter to Santa Claus every year that was like the letters his wealthy cousins wrote. Glenn was a poor farmer's son who never got anything but apples and oranges, even though he asked Santa for exactly the same thing his wealthy cousins got. And every year, Glenn would go out behind the barn and cry. One year, his cousin wanted a brand-new bicycle and Glenn wanted a brand-new bicycle, and as usual, the cousin got it and Glenn didn't. He went out behind the barn and said, "Okay Santa, if that's the way you want to play."

He went on to complete the story by saying, "And on that day, I decided to become my own Santa Claus." He challenged viewers to be their own Santa Claus. You know, the first ten or twenty times I watched that movie I didn't think too much about it. I thought it was a story, I thought he made a good point, and I went on. That was November of 1972.

Two weeks later, I made a shopping list for Christmas. Like everyone, there were the obligatory "why do I do this every year" people on my list. So I was in the department store, in the men's section, when for some reason the message, "Be your own Santa Claus" popped into my mind. And so the first gift I bought was something nice and expensive – for myself – because I deserved it.

"What the heck?" I said to myself. "I'm Santa Claus." And from that day, I have continued to be my own Santa Claus. Cool things have resulted.

- **Christmas for me is no longer just December 25th. It's any day I choose. What the heck, I'm Santa Claus.**

- **I can change any mood I'm in by buying myself a present. That's one of the privileges of being Santa Claus.**

- **I'm celebrating!**

In the spirit of passing down messages that can affect others forever, and with the hope for you to make faster, easier, bigger sales, I'm challenging you to become your own Santa Claus.

NOTE: For those of you fortunate enough to be parents, there's not much of a transition involved, because for your children, young and old, you already are Santa Claus.

Let me be a little more specific. Let me help you in your transition.

Here (in no particular order) are some gifts I would like you to give yourself. Some of them cost money, some of them are free. (As usual, the best ones are free. But all of them will help you to strengthen your belief in yourself and make you a better person.)

1. Give yourself the gift of learning. Something new every day. Resolve that you will buy and read, study and put into practice, one book each month.

2. Give yourself the gift of making an achievable game plan to become a better person, not just a better salesperson. Shape your philosophy and your attitude, Santa, so that your actions will have purpose.

3. Give yourself more sales by providing business gifts for others that help them build their business, not expand their waistline. People don't want food as much as they want new business.

4. Give yourself the gift of something fun. I buy art that's fun and funny. I hang it where I can see it every day. It keeps me smiling all the time. And others smile when they see it. By giving yourself fun, you are also creating an atmosphere of fun that rubs off on others. That's the spirit of fun that Santa himself would endorse.

4.5 Count your blessings. Not just on holidays. Count them every day. Naughty or nice, everyone has blessings. Far fewer count them. Far fewer even recognize that they are the key to personal success and fulfillment.

Okay Santa, I've given you the challenge. Your job is to put the suit on and live the part.

HERE'S THE BEST PART: You will develop the passion that will make you more sales, while your competition gets what they deserve for Christmas – coal. Ho, Ho, Ho!

Your Sales Voice.
What Is It Saying to You?
What Is It Saying to Others?

I was at Washburn University in Topeka, Kansas, giving a seminar sponsored by Sales & Marketing Executives International. I had an informal logistics meeting with some of the association members before the event when Jamie, the young woman who directed me to my preparation room, talked to me about her career. I asked her what she was seeking to become.

Her response startled me. She said, "I'm still trying to find my voice."

I was taken aback because I expected some alternate career choice, or something along the lines of "make a lot of money," or "get a job in event planning." But no, she was seeking something much higher.

Jamie was seeking to gain control of her self and her power first, and find her career path second. We talked about "voice" for a while, and I began to type in order to capture the thoughts.

What came out of the brief conversation will benefit you and your career, and help you understand who you are and who you seek to become.

Jamie was looking for her voice to come from something she believed in that would make her voice stronger. More resonant, more powerful, and more believable.

How do you speak?

Not just the words, the voice that you project. Your voice is a statement and picture of your character, your poise, and your persona. It's a statement of belief, confidence, and personal power.

Where does your voice come from? How do you "find" it? And once you do, how do you master it?

BE AWARE: Your voice has nothing to do with your selling skills or your product knowledge. Your voice is way beyond that.

GOOD NEWS: You don't have to look far. Most of your voice is right at the tip of your tongue. The rest of it is mental and emotional.

ANSWER: It STARTS with your inner voice. It's the language you speak to yourself BEFORE you say a word.

Your voice becomes yours, and authentically yours, when you...

- **Do what you believe in.**
- **Do what you're passionate about.**
- **Work in your chosen field.**
- **Find your calling.**
- **Discover something you feel you were made or born to do.**
- **Do something you love.**

EASY WAY TO START THE DISCOVERY: Write down the hobby or sport you love best, or the sporting event you go to because you love to see your team play and cheer them on.

My friend, Hall of Fame baseball player Dave Winfield, said it as simply and as completely as I have ever heard it, "I loved baseball and baseball loved me back."

Here are the elements of voice:

- **You have decided to pursue your chosen path.**
- **You have belief in who you are.**
- **You have belief in what you do.**
- **You have a desire to succeed.**
- **You're personally prepared – attitude, enthusiasm, friendliness, and ideas.**
- **You maintain self-confidence that comes from your heart, not from your head.**
- **Your enthusiasm is real.**

- **Your sincerity is evident.**
- **You're eager to master every aspect of what you do.**
- **Your passion is contagious.**
- **Your moxie engages others.**
- **Your desire to improve is never ending.**
- **You love what you do.**

NOTE WELL: Your voice is not about how to make sales faster – your voice is how to make sales forever. For your voice to appear, you must possess ALL of these elements. Most people have a "weak" voice because they don't love what they do, or lack sincerity, or they don't fully believe in themselves, their company, or their product.

SUCCESS ACTION: Record your spoken voice ONCE A WEEK, and listen to it actively – which means take notes. By listening to yourself – arguably one of the toughest things on the planet to do – you will gain a true picture of where you are right now. Your jumping-off point.

And for those of you living in the dark ages still trying to "find the pain" in your sales presentation, just record and listen to yourself – THAT'S the pain. The real pain of selling is listening to your voice trying to make a sale – it's also funny as hell.

You'll know your voice when you hear it. It will speak to you before you ever say a word.

IF YOU BREAK THE LAW: Your sales numbers will tell you if you are a believer or not. If you break the law of belief, and self-belief, your numbers will be mediocre. And worse, you'll be blaming everybody else and their dog for why you can't sell more.

The reality is, you have to believe more.

It never ceases to amaze me how many salespeople complain that their product is becoming a commodity, that if they don't have the lowest price they don't win the sale, and that their company doesn't support them enough in their sales role. The remedy, if you're really looking for one, is two words: TAKE RESPONSIBILITY.

IF YOU FOLLOW THE LAW: Belief leads to sales. There is no better way to explain it. And the best part is: belief is self-imposed. It's genuine self-motivation. If you really want to believe, you will become a believer in every aspect of your career and your life. Not only will it be self-evident, it will also be transferable. Your customers will feel your belief. It will make them believers.

Belief creates the passion that allows your presentation to be both understandable and purchasable.

When you have true belief in your company, product, self, differentiation, and deep belief that the customer is better off having purchased from you, you will march to success.

CAUTION: Too many salespeople (not you of course) will tell me that they believe in their product. That is not enough. Belief must be total and deep in order to be transferable. It's not just that you believe; it's can you get others to believe.

KEY TO IMPLEMENTATION: To gain a better understanding of what it takes to be a believer, you must first ask yourself "why." Why do you believe in your company, your product, your service, and yourself? Why do you believe you can differentiate? Why do you believe your customer is better off having purchased from you? Write the answers down. Expand on them. Once you tell yourself why you believe, you can begin strengthening those beliefs from within.

Unbreakable Law

4

EMPLOY HUMOR

CHALLENGE

How funny or humorous are you? How important is humor in sales?
How important is humor in life?

HERE'S THE DEAL: Humor is a science – you can study it, learn it, even
practice it. But before you can employ humor, you have to know when to
use it, how to use it, and what is appropriate.

A Lesson from a Laugh.
Listen to This One.

Ho, ho, ho!

No, it's not Christmas. But jolly is always in season. Some people look at it as a "laugh." I look at it as a learning device, listening tool, attention grabber, self healer, powerful selling tool, and – of course – fun.

An airline flight attendant from Alaska Airlines started his "flight safety announcements" with the statement, "Welcome to Alaska Airlines Flight 320 to San Francisco. If you're not headed to San Francisco, now would be a great time to get off the plane, and one of our friendly gate agents will steer you in the right direction."

I was smiling – so were the rest of the passengers. I was listening – so were the rest of the passengers.

"My name is Mark, I'm the lead flight attendant." He continued, "My ex-wife Sandra, and her new boyfriend, Bill, will be serving you in the back cabin today. This should make for an interesting flight." Now I was laughing (and I was listening) and so was every passenger on the plane. And I listened to EVERY WORD he said from then on.

I fly on airplanes more than 200 times a year, and I NEVER listen to the safety instructions. Oh, I hear them mumbling, but I don't pay attention.

This flight was different. After the first joke, I was listening for the next joke (and to the instructions). This guy was genuinely funny.

The object of the safety instructions, or any oral communication, is to get people to LISTEN. Otherwise, why have them? When you see the way safety instructions are given on an airplane, you howl.

One attendant hides behind a wall and reads a script in a monotone, while another robotically goes through the motions of pantomiming what the other has said. It's a joke – but a pathetic one, not a funny one. No one listens.

On the newer planes, they now have safety videos where one person of every race creed and religious orientation is in each scene, and all of them are plastic (with a white male pilot, of course). This technological innovation does have one thing in common with its human predecessor – no one pays attention. It's dull and there's no compelling reason to listen. In the beginning they beg you to pay attention to this *important* safety announcement. No one does – not even the flight crew.

What's going on in your world?

- **Are people listening to you? Are you sure?**
- **Are they listening to your presentation? Are you sure?**
- **Are they paying attention to your important communications? Are you sure?**

MAJOR CLUE: How much humor is in your communication?

Here's the rule:
Laughter leads to listening.

Whatever you say AFTER you say something funny will be heard and remembered ten times more than when you drone on and "think" or "expect" that others hear it – much less are listening. In short, laughter leads to listening and creates the highest listening environment.

Why does laughter make people listen better? Easy – people would rather be laughing. After the first laugh you want, maybe even expect, another. I wasn't disappointed with that Alaska flight attendant. After the first round of laughs he continued: "If you're caught smoking, we throw you off the plane immediately. And for those of you who brought a TV with you on board, it will not work." Then he gave the announcement about smoking and electronic devices. Perfect. Laugh, then listen. Every person on the plane was paying complete attention.

What can the power of laughter do for you and your sales? Listen up (please pay attention, this is REALLY, REALLY important). After laughter, the prospect is listening, the prospect is more "in the mood" to buy, and the prospect is on the edge of his seat listening for what's next.

"Funny" bridges the gap between professional and friendly.

Got humor?

To get a laugh, or a bunch of laughs, here are 3.5 things to do:

1. **Test your humor on a friend to be sure it's funny before you say it.**

2. **Make sure the laugh is at your own expense, not at someone else's.**

3. **Not funny? Study humor.**

3.5 **Timing is everything. Study comedians. They know HOW and WHEN to deliver a punch line, and how long to pause.**

Beyond the listening and the understanding by the prospect, the most powerful, unspoken part of laughter is that it's tacit approval. A prospect's laugh is a form of personal agreement. Once you get tacit approval (i.e., they like you), then all you need is verbal approval, and you have the order. Then the joke is on the competition.

Ho, ho, ho!

IF YOU BREAK THE LAW: Without humor, there's an invisible barrier between getting to know someone on the surface and getting to know someone on a deeper level.

Humor breaks the ice, creates mutual laughter, and generates a different atmosphere in the room – a lighter, friendlier atmosphere. The omission of humor in any given situation may preclude you from having a true understanding of the person you're talking to.

IF YOU FOLLOW THE LAW: When you employ humor, you create a friendly, relaxed buying atmosphere. Following the law of humor means that you have not made some kind of joke at the expense of others. You haven't created an uncomfortable feeling based on what you've talked about, or joked about. Following the law of humor means that you have collected your stories, tried them out privately, and feel comfortable that they will set the right tone. An ongoing natural sense of humor helps build and strengthen your relationships.

CAUTION: There's a huge difference between jokes and humor. Jokes have no place in a sales conversation, especially if the prospective customer has heard it before, and may potentially be offended by it. Either way, jokes lose. Funny stories? Perfect!

AHA! Everyone wants to, and loves to, laugh. The question is: are you prepared to make laughter happen?

AHA! Humor is the bridge between professional and friendly. Humor is the link to personal and business rapport.

At the end of humor is the height of listening. The other person always wants to hear what's next.

AHA! I use humor every day because it helps me keep my mood both lighthearted and positive. I have also found over a forty-year period of time that humor (not jokes) is the basis for mutual understanding. Something as simple as laughter can immediately bring warmth into a conversation and create a connection that no amount of professionalism can duplicate.

Humor creates relaxation in a meeting. Humor leads to insight. Humor leads to sales.

Twenty years ago I wrote: "If you can make 'em laugh, you can make 'em buy." That quote will stand true the next 100 years.

KEY TO IMPLEMENTATION: Begin collecting and documenting funny things that happened to you. Try to determine how they have related to your life and your career. Try to determine how transferable they might be in a selling situation, and make certain that it is humor that keeps you on the same page. If you both have kids, kid humor. If you both like sports, sports humor. You get the idea. Have a spirited laugh about something you both have in common. The prospect will like you better, and you will love the purchase order.

You cannot deny the power of laughter as a universal bond from human to human and from human to sales order form.

JEFFREY GITOMER

5

BUILD YOUR OWN BRAND

CHALLENGE

PICTURE THIS: You just got laid off from a job you've had for the past five years. Now what? Obviously the answer is find a job – a great job – as fast as you can. One that pays more than your old job so you can call your boss and tell him or her to stick it.

BUT THE QUESTION REALLY IS: Who are you? If you're going to apply for a new job, you probably think you need to update your resume. Are you kidding me? I mean are you serious? Resume? Dude, the days of only having a resume are over. Social media, personal brand, and reputation have taken over – forever. If you come to me looking for a job, I don't care about your resume and I don't care about your references. Do you honestly think I am going to call your high school track coach or a college professor who thinks you're a great guy?

Heck no! I'll just look you up on Google. I'm going to see if you have a Twitter account. I want to see how many connections you have on LinkedIn. I'm gonna look for your blog and your website. Got a YouTube channel?

The time to build your brand is while you're working, so that if you do lose your job or even decide to change jobs, your personal brand will land you a better job.

NOW PICTURE THIS: You have to make a presentation to a huge customer, against two competitors. You have a one-hour meeting scheduled with three decision makers. You Google the company, and then you Google the three decision makers. You try to be as prepared as humanly possible. Meanwhile, your customer is "Googling" you. They're finding out everything they can about who you are as a person. If your personal brand is weaker than your competition's, and your online reputation is weaker than your competition's, you walk into the meeting in an inferior position before you even start. Reason? You're watching television at night instead of building your brand.

In the old days you could get away with being a company man. Today you better be your own man or woman.

You better have your own brand and your own reputation because it gets there way before you do, and sets the tone for the mutual respect you're hoping for.

What Does "Branding" Mean to You?

Growing up in the '50s and '60s, I still have a vision of hot branding irons in a coal or wood fire, and some rancher roping a steer or a horse and pressing the red hot branding iron against its skin, to make sure the name of their ranch was branded on the animal.

OUCH! But the brand was on the animal forever.

In today's marketplace, that's what all brands seek to achieve. They want their name or product emblazoned on the mind of the buyer *permanently*.

ONE PROBLEM: Just because you "know the brand" or "remember the brand" does not mean you're going to BUY it. And the reality is if I know it and recognize it, but I don't buy it, then all the money spent on branding is wasted. OUCH!

The problem rests with marketing and advertising people – they're not salespeople. They know everything in the world about exposure and branding, but jack about *making* the sale.

The power of marketing is the conversion of awareness and recognition into a purchase. *Hey, you over there in marketing. You remember profit, don't you?*

NOTE: If you're spending to become known, you better be able to back it up once the potential customer decides to reach out and touch you.

Here are the "be's" of branding to make sales faster, easier, and bigger:

- Be likeable.
- Be believable.
- Be available.
- Be attractive.
- Be friendly.

- Be service-oriented.
- Be first-class.
- Be consistent.
- Be reputable.
- Be desirable.
- Be trustworthy.
- Be top quality.
- Be easy to do business with.
- Be "buzzable." (Are they "spreading the word?")

SECRET: Be part of a sales team that can convey and convert the branding message in terms of the buyer (the user, the customer), so they are compelled to buy.

When someone sees your brand or your ad, what do you want them to think? *What are they thinking now?*

When someone talks about your brand, what do you want them to say? *What are they saying now?*

When someone sees your ad or your product, what do you want them to do? *What are they doing now?*

Your answers to those six questions are the reality of your brand, your reputation, and your ability to make sales.

LESSON: With all the branding hoopla and information in the marketplace, you would think it would be difficult to make a statement or a claim that hasn't been said or done before. You would be wrong.

If you're looking to brand, get known, build a reputation, AND make sales, you only have to:

- **Study your local market.**
- **Look at the global market for other ideas.**
- **Listen to the voice of your present customers.**

- Study creativity.

- Build a customer-focused message.

- Back it with quality and deeds.

- Dedicate your people to friendly service.

- Create the atmosphere where people want to, and are able to, BUY.

Light the fire. Get the branding iron hot. Burn your brand on the mind and wallet of your customer. But be prepared to sell when they get there – or be prepared to lose to someone who is.

Brand is not just about becoming known and shouting your name.

You have to back it up with the elements of quality, consistency, customer focus, customer help, response, service, and customer attraction. Then throw in a dose of fun so that the customer BUYS!

BONUS: If you're able to brand AND sell, your competition will hate your guts. What could be better than that?

Your customer wants to do business with a somebody not a nobody.

JEFFREY GITOMER

Are You the Dominant Brand, or Is Your Brand Bland?

What's the difference between you and your competition?

Are you different from your competition, or you just THINK you are? Are you different from your competition, or you just tell customers and prospects you are? Or are you different from your competition, *and others CLEARLY perceive you as both different and better?*

REALITY: It's not what you think or believe, it's what your customers do and say.

REALITY: If I ask you what the difference is between you and your prime competitor, and your answer is "our people" or "me," you're in serious trouble.

REALITY: If you asked your customer what the difference is, what would they say? "Cheaper." "Closer to my home." "I dunno, been using them for years." "Six of one – half a dozen of the other." You're in trouble.

Beyond your brand, your reputation is a reality check of where you actually are versus where you think you are:

- **What's your customer's perception of your reputation?** The answer doesn't come from a satisfaction survey or a phone interview. The answer comes from a face-to-face talk when you ask 100 of your customers what they really think of you, and why they buy.

- **What's your social reputation?** As posted on your business Facebook page by your customer, or as recommended by customers on their social media accounts?

- **What's your industry reputation?** How do both leaders and vendors perceive you in your industry?

- **What's your community reputation?** If you had a community town hall meeting, what would they say about you?

Here are more painful brand-related questions to ask yourself:

- **What am I doing to build my brand?**

- **What am I doing to innovate my products or services?**

- **What am I doing to change or enhance my customer's experience?**

Apple has an incredible brand – one of the most recognizable in the world. You've seen their ads – funny, compelling, and authentic. And they're the classic example of a brand with products that back it up.

Their retail stores match their marketing. Attractive and compelling products with helpful, smart workers. And it's easy to make a purchase. To make CERTAIN their branding message reaches the consumer in a positive way, they put their own salespeople in other retail outlets to be certain the customer has all the information needed to make an intelligent decision.

Apple's competition is "me too," and often mentions Apple in their ads. If you brag that you're "just like Apple," then personally I want Apple. The experience I have in Apple stores is in perfect harmony with the brand they're portraying.

In the computer industry, the smart phone industry, the tablet industry, and the music player industry, only Apple stands alone not comparing themselves to other products, unless it's a joke. They don't have to talk about their competition – Apple is the innovator. And they do it at their price.

What's up in your world? Are you the dominant brand? Are you Amazon? eBay? Jello? Kleenex? Kellogg's Corn Flakes? Jacuzzi?

HARD QUESTION: Are you comparing your products to the competition, or differentiating yourself from the competition?

HARD QUESTION: Are you trying to justify price, or does your quality reputation precede you?

OUCH QUESTION: Is your brand, product, or service superior in the marketplace, but you haven't yet elevated your personal brand to that position of dominance?

NOTE WELL: Then there are the brands that USED to be #1 and have fallen to #2 or lower. Either by inferior products, inferior service, or disgraced reputation. Blackberry, American Airlines, Microsoft, and Tiger Woods to name a few.

Here are 5.5 interviews you need to do to get the TRUTH from people who are willing to give it to you. In order to get better tomorrow, you gotta know where you are today.

1. **Interview customers who said no to you.** They'll tell you why they chose someone else.

2. **Interview customers who left you.** They'll tell you why, and how to improve.

3. **Interview customers who love you.** They'll tell you the good stuff.

4. **Interview loyal employees.** They'll tell you why they love you.

5. **Interview departed employees.** They'll tell you why they left you.

5.5 **Interview industry leaders.** They'll give you the big picture you may not be able to see.

CAUTION: Leave PR, marketing, and advertising out of the equation, or you may NEVER get to the truth. My recommendation is to hire an outside branding company, and at least get a new perspective from the outside world (your customers and the marketplace) *and* the inside world (your people).

After your interviews, here's what to do:

- **Be realistic about outside opinions and how you can create improvement.**

- **Create internal excitement about innovation and new ideas.**

- **Train and teach attitude, self-belief, and creativity.**

- **Give people paid days off just to think and create.**

- **Create a sense of self-pride in your people by listening to their thoughts and ideas.**

- **Praise and implement new ideas.**

RESULT: A new, market-dominant, more profitable you.

In today's volatile global marketplace, the only brand you can be certain of is your own.

JEFFREY GITOMER

Your Name Matters to Your Prospects. Or Does It?

Here is a question I've been asked more than a hundred times in one form or another: How do I make a (better) name for myself?

Here is the premise, the definition, and the answer:

In sales it's not who you know; in sales it's who knows you.

The challenge is not just making a name for yourself or building your brand; it's building the components that generate that name.

How do you achieve more recognition, more notoriety, and a better reputation in your market and your community? Those are the *elements* that lead to a better name. And to be clear, I'm talking about a better name for both company and individual.

There are no easy answers. And there are very few answers that don't require commitment, planning, and work – hard work.

GOOD NEWS: Most salespeople are not willing to do the hard work it takes to make selling easy. BUT, if you're willing, you automatically move to the top 10%. And if you execute, you're in the top 5%.

MAJOR CLUE: How do you tell the whiners from the winners? The whiners are complaining about everything and they're worried about "losing their job." The winners are planning to win, believing they'll win, and taking action. *Which are you?*

BETTER NEWS: When the economy is in transition (that's a nice way to put it, isn't it?), it's the easiest time for you to make a change, and begin to execute new ideas.

There are things you must begin to put in place now. Below are the actions that lead to long-term name building that must be implemented and built upon. NONE of these elements are "do now and forget about." Rather, they are "do now, do tomorrow, and do forever."

- **Create your own weekly e-zine that features valuable information and highlights your customers.** Look at my weekly email magazine, *Sales Caffeine*, as an example. Go to www.salescaffeine.com and read about it. Look at an issue and emulate the process in your weekly e-zine.

- **Register www.(yourname).com today. It's only ten bucks.** If it's taken, put "The Great" or "the one and only" in front of it. Get your web address, your URL address, registered TODAY. The world is on the web. The Internet is NEVER going away. It's the growth and the future of commerce. Be on it, or be gone.

- **Invest in a small but powerful website that looks like something people would read, admire, tell others about, and maybe even buy from.** Start with a one-page website that talks about "how I treat my customers." Make a list of the ten most valuable things you are dedicated to. Later you can add more pages, pictures, graphics, and pizzazz. But start small and be compelling.

- **Be 1,000% more proactive.** This means hitting both the phone and the send button. Make ten calls a day that have value, and send twenty-five emails that have meaning to the recipient. Build relationships and earn referrals.

- **Write something that puts you in front of customers and prospects.** Put an article in your trade publication or your chamber of commerce magazine. Writing leads to recognition. Writing positions you as an expert and an authority.

- **Blog to show your human side.** Make your blog a family affair. Show who you are, your personality, your passion, and your fun.

- **YouTube.** Video your value proposition. Video your testimonials. Video your philosophy of sales and service. Post your videos on YouTube. Your customers and prospects will find them, and find you more attractive than your (lazy) competitors.

- **Get involved in your community.** Pick one charity or one civic organization to get involved with. Assert leadership.

- **Get Google-able.** *WAKE UP, Sparky!* Your customer is "Googling" you, just like you are Googling them. Your one-page website, your e-zine, your article, your speech, and your community involvement will bring your name and your company's name to the top of the Google pile.

- **Be a value provider – not a beggar, a solicitor, or a salesman.** People will BUY if they perceive your value. And they will spread the word about your name and your brand.

TIME IS YOUR FRIEND: Be patient with it. Invest in it. Use it to your best advantage. To really build a name for yourself, it takes time. Lots of it. It takes commitment. Lots of it. And, it takes consistency.

YOUR NAME MEANS EVERYTHING: Name and reputation are intertwined. Those who become valuable to their customers, their marketplace, and their community are the ones who win short term and long term.

WHAT ARE PEOPLE SAYING ABOUT YOU? When someone says your name, they're also going to say one of five things about you: something great, something good, nothing, something bad, or something real bad. Whatever they say determines your fate.

If you want to build name recognition, and a great reputation, you have to dedicate yourself to the long-term process and the short-term work.

Free GitBit... Want my secret for long-term name recognition? Go to www.gitomer.com and enter the word NAME in the GitBit box.

IF YOU BREAK THE LAW: A simple, sixty-second online search will tell me whether you have built your own brand – or not. Personal brand is not a luxury, and it's not just for people who have big money. A personal brand is for everybody. You included. If you haven't built your own brand, you create an immediate deficit position as you walk into a sales call. It creates a long list of excuses, none of which are valid. The customer has tried to find out information about you, and none of it exists. If you have no personal brand, you have to become defensive about who you aren't instead of proud of who you are. The longer you wait to build your brand, the more opportunity your well-branded competition has to win the sale.

IF YOU FOLLOW THE LAW: Building your own brand will pay dividends based on its perceived value and how it is combined with your personal reputation. Potential customers don't just vet your company and your product – they're vetting you... and they're doing it way before you ever walk in the door.

Your personal brand will be the open door to getting information that will help you land the sale. The reason you're getting the information is that you've already built reputation and trust with your potential customers when they asked their colleagues about you or searched for you online.

CAUTION AND CHALLENGE: Your personal brand must be built out all the way. It must be in complete harmony with your reputation so that one augments and supplements the other. It has to contain every aspect of social media including a YouTube channel with valuable information AND testimonials. Several of your customers could record a YouTube video that extols your virtues both as a salesperson and a human being. You should also have a blog that posts customer value-based information.

AHA! Everyone has a personal brand. The only question is, are you in charge of yours, are you building yours, or are you leaving it to chance?

AHA! Your brand is a combination of the actions you take to build it, how you promote yourself, your past history of success, and your reputation.

AHA! Personal brand excellence is no longer an option, it's an imperative.

AHA! The cool part about a personal brand is that it instills pride and self-confidence. You know what someone's going to find when they check you out. They're going to be impressed, and that impression will lead to a sale.

KEY TO IMPLEMENTATION: Start your blog today. Make it a combination of posts about your marketplace (and how your customers can benefit from the product or service you sell) and your personal interests. Post on your blog AT LEAST once a week. Let everyone on your email mailing list know about each time you post, and ask them to subscribe. If it's good, they will. And if it's real good, they'll tell their friends.

Your value-based information, your exceptional service, and your quality of product and person determine your brand, your name, and your fate.

JEFFREY GITOMER

EARN REPUTATION

CHALLENGE

Your sales reputation has five elements: Reputation of your company, reputation of your product, reputation of your service, reputation of the type of people you do business with, and your personal reputation.

Obviously, your personal reputation is at the forefront. But the other four are undeniably important to your overall chances for success. Building a reputation can take years; losing your reputation can take minutes. This law presents the challenge of both building it and preserving it. At the core of your reputation are your ethics, your integrity, your ability to do the right thing all the time, and your truth. Powerful challenge. More than powerful reward.

Reputation is the Sister of Branding. And Vice-Versa.

Reputation is the foundation by which brands grow or die.

Your reputation is what people say about you.

- **How you did it.**
- **What you did about it.**
- **How you served.**
- **What their experience was.**
- **And whether or not they will recommend you.**

Your brand is built and enhanced by your reputation.

BRAND IS THE ITEM, THE COMPANY, THE NAME, OR THE PERSON. Chevrolet, Kleenex, iPhone, Apple, Microsoft, Jell-O, Wheaties, Kim Kardashian, Joe DiMaggio, Pete Rose.

REPUTATION IS WHAT PEOPLE SAY, POST, TWEET, AND YOUTUBE ABOUT THE BRAND. It's how they talk about the item, the company, the name, or the person.

Once established, brand and reputation become closer and closer, but they are never the same. Your brand rises and falls, lives and breathes, or lives and dies by your reputation.

As you're working to build your personal brand and earn reputation, study others – both successful and failed. Write down the elements of their success. Document why they failed. Use those insights as your guideline for which elements to follow or avoid.

One thing is certain about both brand and reputation – they are built slowly over time. And once established, they must be guarded, enhanced, and valued. Build your brand and earn your reputation. Guard them as your most valuable possessions.

Want to Have a Great Reputation? Earn It!

Your reputation precedes you. Your reputation creates or destroys sales. What's yours?

With the onslaught of social media, good and bad actions and comments relating to quality of product, quality of service, and quality of experience are at the forefront of corporate awareness.

Many companies are reluctant to get into social media out of fear their customers will say or post negative things about them.

REALITY: Those companies and their leaders are "socially" unaware that the customer is going to post those feelings anyway.

WORSE REALITY: Many companies are under the influence of shallow lawyers who warn executives the sky is falling if someone tweets.

WORST REALITY: Even more ridiculous are the companies that "forbid" the use of social media at work based on the fear their employees will waste their time searching for their old high school romance.

NEWS ALERT: Social media – or business social media (as I prefer to refer to it) – is now a mainstay.

The floodgates of social freedom are reshaping the world and at the same time reshaping – or at least redefining – your company, your product, your service, and your people through the voice of your customers.

And social media, when combined with word-of-mouth advertising and stories that may appear online or in print, determines your fate and your future. All of that combines to equal YOUR REPUTATION.

Another way to look at and define your reputation is the state or status of "becoming known as" or "becoming known for" something.

Here's what to work toward:

1. Become known for doing everything you said you would do – on time or sooner. To have any prayer for a reputation you must be known as a person who does and delivers what you promise. Without this fundamental element, don't bother to read the rest.

2. Become known as friendly and easy to do business with. Customers expect everything and they expect it when they need it – not just when you can offer it. You have to be friendly when you are there and friendly when you are not there. This means easily accessible by telephone and easily accessible by Internet.

3. Become known for being proactively remarkable. When you stand out from other vendors, you will be talked about, and earning a reputation (and a testimonial) will be simple. Being remarkable means going the extra mile and making service the forefront of your business, not an add-on.

4. Become known for providing consistent help. If you get my weekly email magazine, *Sales Caffeine*, you know it is all about sales help. Each week I provide my customers information of value – information that helps them learn and grow. And I do it for free. As a result, my customers and followers are loyal, they think of me often in a positive way, and they proactively send me referrals on a regular basis.

4.5 Become known as someone who gets business for customers. While this is not always possible, I can assure you it is the single most valuable thing you can do to secure loyal relationships, referrals, an incredible reputation, and testimonials that will flow like Niagara Falls. Figure out a way to help your customer by providing them leads, referrals, and networking opportunities so they have an opportunity to get new business.

When you let your positive words and actions speak for themselves, your reputation will rise in the process.

JEFFREY GITOMER

It Was a Chance Meeting.
Or Was It?

I was walking in the parking lot of my local Starbucks in Charlotte, North Carolina, with Gabrielle in my arms, when a guy came over and started to talk to me.

He told me he'd seen me give two different seminars several years ago and asked, "Hey, do you still do seminars?"

I assured him that I still did seminars and that I LOVE doing seminars.

He said that he was hosting a conference in Charlotte for assorted CEOs, and was wondering if I would be interested in speaking to the group.

"HECK YES! I would love to. And in fact, I just published my *Little Book of Leadership*."

He told me there was another big meeting that would take place in the fall, and he would recommend me for that one as well. I gave him my coin card and my Philadelphia Phillies-themed business card.

As he smiled, I suggested that he call my office on Monday to speak with Michelle Joyce, our Queen of Events.

He assured me that he would. I also let him know we would send him a seminar kit.

Even though I wanted his business card (badly), it was a Saturday morning and we were both in shorts – so I left it to the gods that he would take the next step and call.

Just after I strapped Gabrielle in her car seat, I turned around to see the man handing me his business card and smiling. YES!

And after my conference call with him on Tuesday, it turns out this was a major business opportunity for my company.

That's the end of the story – for now.

Coincidence? Chance meeting? Serendipity? My personal philosophy and belief is there are no accidents, but that may be the result of growing up as an idealist in the '60s.

THE BIG QUESTION IS: What led up to the interaction?

My years of hard work, my reputation, my writing, my seminars, and my books created the opportunity for that meeting.

I was both recognizable and attractive. I was both available and approachable. I was memorable enough to spur an action on the part of the person who recognized me.

What would have happened if that person bumped into you at your Starbucks on a Saturday morning?

Rather than me tell you what you probably already know, let me ask a series of questions that will hopefully lead you to take actions toward reputation, recognition, and approachability:

- **When you Google yourself, does your presence occupy at least the first page?**
- **Are your social media messages getting responses?**
- **Are people proactively posting on your Facebook page about how much they enjoy you and are inspired by you?**
- **Are your tweets being re-tweeted?**
- **Are you writing in a manner that is attracting others?**
- **Are you speaking at trade shows in order to gain prospective customers?**
- **Are you doing anything that your competition is NOT doing in order to appear different from them and more valuable than they are?**
- **Are you building your personal brand, or are you just tagging along with your company's brand and product?**

These are not just "ouch" questions; they're also success, life, and reputation questions. And, in the end, these are legacy questions.

If you are going to win in sales, you have to be a dominant player with an impeccable reputation, not just a sales rep.

The guy in Starbucks didn't just recognize me, he remembered me. And our encounter didn't just happen; I've spent the last thirty-five years making it happen. I'm writing this to you and for you so that you may become inspired to dedicate yourself to next-level achievement.

In my years of experience, I have discovered that:

- **More salespeople complain about "what isn't" rather than talk about what's possible.**

- **More salespeople whine about their price or the economy rather than take aggressive action to build awareness and value in the heart of their customer.**

My heart is in selling. My heart is in writing. My heart is in giving memorable presentations. My heart is in providing value to existing and prospective customers.

Where is your heart? What are you determined to do? What are you dedicated to do? How much time are you dedicating to that determination?

My meeting on Saturday had NOTHING to do with luck. Thirty years ago, Melvin Green, one of my mentors, taught me, "Hard work makes luck."

How lucky are you?

IF YOU BREAK THE LAW: The loss of reputation is easy to define but often impossible to recover from: lack of promise fulfillment; lack of quality of product; slow, poor, or rude service; poor ethics; unscrupulous or dishonest business practices; low reliability. And with the advent and omnipresence of the Internet, you can no longer hide your indiscretions. RESULT: Silent rejection. Avoidance.

IF YOU FOLLOW THE LAW: Reputation will create the real law of attraction. When you have earned a great reputation, your exposure will expand exponentially. Both people and businesses will want to connect with you, build a relationship with you, and buy from you. Having a great reputation also builds personal pride and self-confidence. You know when you enter any meeting or any networking event, people will want to talk to you and engage you. Reputation is a vital part of your success definition. Businesses that succeed, but have an iffy reputation, eventually fade away or crumble.

CAUTION AND CHALLENGE: Reputation is not a one-time thing. It takes consistent actions and expressions to maintain it and build it.

Everything from the way you conduct your business to the way you conduct yourself, to your social media, and even your Wikipedia page, adds to or subtracts from the reputation you have worked so hard to gain. Act on it and guard it.

CAUTION AND CHALLENGE: At some point, you may lose your reputation or have someone put a dent in it. This is where your business and personal resilience are called to action.

I find it interesting that most people will not face their challenges early enough. There is defensiveness and denial, followed by the inevitability of confession. (It's probably easiest to see in politicians, because they're so visible.)

When you see it in others it's almost pathetic, but it's much more difficult to look in the mirror and see it.

HERE'S THE RULE: The earlier you address damage to your reputation, the easier it is to recover from it. And vice versa.

AHA! Like it or not, Mother Google is more powerful than you are when it comes to your reputation. And when it comes to the sale, nothing is more profitable than your reputation.

AHA! Your company's reputation pales in comparison to your reputation.

AHA! Your words, actions, and deeds create your reputation – but your biggest responsibility is to protect it and grow it.

AHA! Your reputation often arrives way before you do.

AHA! Your customer Googles you, just like you Google them.

KEY TO IMPLEMENTATION: Make a list of what you want to be known for and known as. Compare that to what shows up when you Google yourself. Your game plan will be self-evident from there. If you're looking to become someone better and become known for something at which you excel – and those elements don't appear in a Google search – make it your goal to take specific actions until they do appear.

Sales reps make quota. Dominant players don't worry about quota – they blow it away. And dominant players gain recognition, and build reputation, based on hard work.

JEFFREY GITOMER

BE ASSERTIVE AND PERSISTENT

CHALLENGE

The age-old question in sales is: "Should I, or shouldn't I?" This question refers to almost every action a salesperson might take, but it is especially common in the areas of leaving a message, asking for the sale, or when is the best time to follow up. There is no one best answer to any of these situations, but my challenge is: more than you dare. You are about to get a lesson that redefines persistence. It challenges you to build your own self-confidence through attitude, belief, and preparation. And provides answers you can implement and bank on. It revolves around one word: assertive.

Are You Passive, Aggressive, or Assertive? Only One Way Wins.

Salespeople get a bad rap for trying to sell too hard.

You've heard the term "pushy salesman" or "aggressive salesperson" or even "obnoxious salesman." How do those phrases make you feel?

And salespeople go to great lengths to NOT be perceived as pushy, or aggressive, or obnoxious – so they (maybe you) go to the opposite end of the spectrum and try to become or be known as professional.

BEWARE AND BE AWARE: A professional sales call is okay, but boring. Professional meetings typically have no outcome. Or worse, they result in never-ending follow-up, void of sales. Not good.

Here's a good way to think about professionalism: your customer must *perceive* you as a professional person. It's more of a look on your part, and a perception on the part of the customer.

In today's world of selling, professionalism is a given. Your words, actions, and deeds take over from there.

Professionalism is not bad, but professionalism alone will not net sales.

Between pushy, aggressive, obnoxious, and professional lies a middle ground – a ground where sales are made. It's known as *assertive.*

CAUTION: Assertiveness is not a word – it's a strategy and a style.

It's not just "a way in which you conduct yourself." Rather, it's a full-blown strategy that has elements to master long before assertiveness can begin and be accepted as a style of selling.

BEWARE AND BE AWARE: Assertiveness is a GOOD style of selling as long as you understand, and have mastered, the elements that make "assertive" acceptable on the part of the customer.

Where does assertiveness come from?

- **The root of assertiveness is belief.** Your belief in what you do, your belief in who you represent, your belief in the products and services that you sell, your belief in yourself, your belief that you can differentiate yourself from your competitor (not compare yourself to), and your *firm* belief that the customer is better off having purchased from you. These are not things you believe in your head. Rather, these are things you must believe in your heart. Deep belief is the first step in creating an assertive process. Until you believe, mediocrity is the norm. Once you believe in your heart, all else is possible.

- **An attitude of positive anticipation.** In order to be assertive, positive attitude or *YES! Attitude* is not enough. You must possess an "attitude of positive anticipation." This means walking into any sales call with a degree of certainty that the outcome will be in your favor. It means having a spirit about you that is easily contagious – a spirit that your customer can catch, and buy.

- **Total preparation is the secret sauce of assertiveness.** This must include customer-focused, pre-call planning as well as creating the objective, the proposed outcome, for a sales call. Most salespeople make the fatal mistake of preparing in terms of themselves (product knowledge, literature, business cards, blah, blah). The reality of total preparation means preparing in terms of the customer FIRST. Their needs, their desires, and their anticipated positive outcomes – their win. If these elements are not an integral part of your preparation, you will lose to someone who has them.

- **The assertive equation must also contain undeniable value in favor of the customer.** This is not just part of preparation. This is also part of the relationships you have built with other customers who are willing to testify on your behalf, and other proof that you have (hopefully in video format) that a prospective customer can relate to, believe in, and as a result, make a purchase.

REALITY: In order to become more assertive, you may have to change some of your present habits or beliefs.

- **It's not about changing your attitude; it's about building your attitude.**
- **It's not about changing your preparation; it's about intensifying your preparation.**
- **It's not about adding value; it's about delivering perceived value.**

BIGGER REALITY: When you have mastered *belief, attitude, preparation,* and *value* as I have just defined them, then and only then can assertiveness and assertive selling *begin* to take place.

BIGGEST REALITY: Incremental growth in belief, attitude, preparation, and value offered will lead to assertive sales calls and an increase in sales.

Your stature is the glue. It's all about:

- **Your quiet self-confidence.**
- **Your surety of knowledge and information that can help your customer.**
- **Your past history of success.**
- **Your possession of undeniable proof.**
- **Your assertive ability to ask your customers to be responsible to their customers and their employees.**

Responsibility is an acceptable and assertive form of accountability.

NOTE WELL: No customer wants to be accountable to a salesperson – but EVERY customer has a MISSION to be responsible to his or her customers and coworkers.

When you combine your belief, your attitude, your preparation, your value, and your assertiveness, the outcome is predictable: more sales.

JEFFREY GITOMER

Assertive Presentation, Persistent Follow-up

Assertive is the best strategy for engaging, establishing control, proving value, creating a buying atmosphere, and forging a relationship.

I define assertiveness as a state of mind and a state of preparation PRIOR to implementation in a sales call.

The two remaining aspects of assertiveness are:

1. **The sales presentation itself.**

2. **The follow-up to the sales call.**

It's interesting that the sales call, the actual presentation, does not require the same amount of assertiveness as the sales follow-up. It's way more difficult to re-engage a prospect and chase down a decision.

However, if you're a great salesperson, an assertive salesperson, follow-up may not be necessary because you have asserted your way to the sale during the presentation.

THE PRESENTATION: When you get in front of a prospective customer, it is imperative that you look impressive and sound impressive.

You know the old saying, "You never have a second chance to make a first impression." You must start in a positive position in order to create a positive outcome.

Assertiveness begins with your eye contact, smile, and handshake. These actions establish you in the mind of the prospect as a person who is both self-assured and happy.

You take a relaxed seat. You accept anything that is offered to you in the way of water or coffee. You put yourself in the lean-forward position. Any tools or equipment you need to make your presentation are in front of you and ready to go. And you immediately begin by discussing anything other than your business and their business.

You begin the business of making friends. You begin the business of creating mutual smiles. You begin talking about them in a way that lets them know you've done your preparation and your homework.

At any moment you can begin to discuss their needs, however, you prefer to discuss their family or their personal interests first.

The segue from rapport building to business discussion requires an assertive thought process. There's no formula, but there is a feeling.

The salesperson's responsibility is to feel when it's right to move forward, and then have the assertive courage to do it.

BEWARE AND BE AWARE: Whoever you're calling on wants to know what's new and what the trends are in THEIR business. If you are able to deliver those during your presentation, I guarantee you'll develop a value-based relationship and have the full attention of the buyer.

The assertive presentation challenges you, the salesperson, to offer a combination of your knowledge as it relates to the customer's needs, as well as a durability to connect both verbally and nonverbally with the person or the group you're addressing.

You'll know your assertive strategy is working when the customer or the prospective customer begins asking questions to get a deeper understanding about your product or service.

These questions change monologue to dialogue and also create the power of engagement, or I should say *assertive engagement.*

At some point you have to complete the transaction.

This means either asking for the sale (an okay part of the assertive process), or using some secondary means to confirm the sale (like scheduling delivery or installation).

Commitment to the order is where the rubber meets the road. If you get the order, it means you've done an assertively great job. If you don't get it, it means you have to lapse into assertive follow-up mode.

FOLLOW-UP: Persistent follow-up will become permissible if asked for, and agreed upon, in advance.

HERE'S HOW: "Mr. Jones, what's the best way for me to stay in touch with you?" "What's your preferred method of communication?" "Is there anyone else I should 'cc' in our communications?" "May I text you?"

These are permission-based questions that tell you where you are in the relationship. If you get a cell phone number and you're permitted to send an occasional text, it means your relationship has reached a solid position.

WHERE'S THE VALUE? If I ask for a "follow-up" appointment, I'll no doubt get some vague runaround. BUT if I offer to come back with some valuable information about his or her business or job function, I'm certain to be granted that appointment.

The dialogue might go something like this, "Mr. Jones, I visit thirty or forty businesses a month. During those visits I don't just sell, I observe. Each month I list two or three 'best practices.' In my follow-up with you, I'll need five minutes to share those practices from the past couple of months. Is that fair enough?"

Heck yes that's fair enough! Your offer to help the customer with his or her business or job function will not just endear you. It will also create the basis of a solid relationship. A value-based relationship. One where assertiveness is actually acceptable.

The ultimate goal beyond a sale is a trusted relationship with your customer. The path to secure that relationship begins with your ability to harness the power of "assertive" in your sales presentation.

IF YOU BREAK THE LAW: It never ceases to amaze me that salespeople want to be the most persistent people on the planet, yet when it comes to the simple act of making a phone call, or leaving a voicemail message, they chicken out. Not being assertive and persistent can cost you opportunities, sales, relationships, and maybe even employment. Why would you RISK not leaving a message, or not making a call, or not following up consistently in order to gain the sale?

IF YOU FOLLOW THE LAW: Persistence and assertiveness are the essence of successful selling, and it's where your ability to complete the sale kicks into its highest gear. Using an assertive approach, and being consistently persistent, will lead you to more sales than you can measure. This law will give you the sales numbers that you are striving for, working hard for, and hoping for. There is no substitute for assertiveness and persistence. And there is no greater reward for proper execution.

CAUTION: The keyword is: RISK. Each time you follow up, each time you press the persistence button, each time you use assertiveness in the selling process, you're taking a risk. The easiest way to overcome this risk is to rethink your own definition of it. Rather than thinking, "If I leave a message I might risk angering the prospective customer," I suggest you think, "If I DON'T leave a message, I risk losing the sale."

Be assertive,
not aggressive.

AHA! Be persistent, with permission in advance. Agree in advance on the how and the when.

AHA! Don't leave messages asking if they've made a decision. Rather, leave messages that have some value to the customer. This way you will never hesitate to leave a message. Reality: This requires creativity and work on the part of the salesperson.

AHA! Persistence using creativity to WOW! the customer and win the sale is the essence of assertiveness.

KEY TO IMPLEMENTATION: In order to win more sales you must "connect the sales cycle." This means you go from one FIRM appointment to another FIRM appointment. Firm appointments are the most powerful, yet often unused follow-up principle. It's a very simple concept and a very simple rule: you never leave an appointment, or hang up the phone, without another firm appointment for the next step in the cycle. This way you are never chasing anyone based on some nebulous promise that they made you. It's always an exact time, date, and place – otherwise you will be forever chasing the prospect, and your tail.

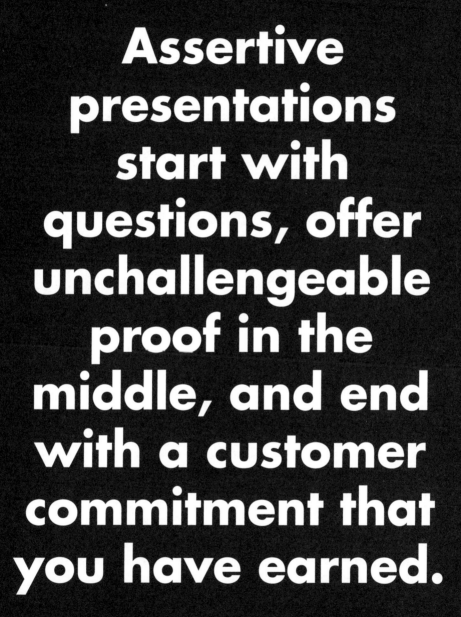

Assertive presentations start with questions, offer unchallengeable proof in the middle, and end with a customer commitment that you have earned.

JEFFREY GITOMER

Unbreakable Law

DEMONSTRATE EXCELLENCE

CHALLENGE

In the early 1980s, Tom Peters and Bob Waterman wrote a benchmark business book called *In Search of Excellence*. According to Peters, excellence was so rare that they had to go in search of it. And when they found it, they talked about it as if it were the Holy Grail.

The book was not only about companies, it also focused on excellent people and excellent execution – individuals who made a difference in their company, their product, their service, and their reputation.

How's your excellence? How dedicated are you to personal excellence? How consistent is your excellent execution?

The answer to these questions will determine both growth and future.

It's Not Being Best – It's Setting the Standard.

When I say the words "set the standard," what comes to your mind?

Personal standards of yours? Standards that your business sets? Standards you have in your mind about other people? Standards you have in your mind about other products?

When you go to a restaurant and order your favorite steak, you'll always recall the one restaurant (especially if it's the one you're in) that had the best steak (or whatever your favorite food was). That restaurant set the standard. All other steaks you will ever eat will be compared to the standard bearer, until one day you may get a better steak, and then that restaurant will become the new standard bearer.

You know and recognize dozens of standard setters in your life – especially when these products or people are amazing and have your undying loyalty, and especially if you proactively refer them. It could be as simple as the best ice cream or the best apple pie. It could be the best dentist or the best chiropractor. It could be the best financial planner.

The best car. The best clothing. The best computer. The best phone. Things that you would never consider doing without.

Whatever those products are, whoever those people are, they set the standard. Your standard.

There are third-party standards...

- **Wilt Chamberlain scored 100 points in a single basketball game. He didn't just set a record. He set the standard.**

- **Abe Lincoln delivered the Gettysburg Address. It wasn't just a speech. He set the standard.**

- **At the steps of the Lincoln Memorial, Martin Luther King, Jr., gave a speech to 500,000 people. It wasn't just a speech. He set the standard.**

The Beatles.

Elvis Presley.

They both set the standard and paved the way for others.

When Wilt Chamberlain set the standard for scoring, it was on March 2, 1962. That standard has endured more than fifty years. Kobe Bryant's 81 points were good, but not as good as Wilt's 100 points – the standard.

Accomplishments are always compared to a standard. Quality is always compared to a standard. Products are always compared to a standard. You know what the best products in your industry are. If you work for that company, you love it and vice versa.

Now that you get the idea of what I'm talking about, let's talk about your business and your career.

What standards are you setting and who are the people involved in setting those standards? Not just in your company, but also in the mind of your customer and in the reputation of your business, in your community, and in your industry.

Your reputation stems from what others think about you and say about you. In today's world, it's what others post online about you.

Reputation comes from setting standards in service, quality of product, consistency, and availability.

You may think of it as "best." But there's a big difference between bragging about the fact you are the "best" and "I set the standard."

There are many products in which you can argue "who is best."

But there's often an obvious winner. German automobile engineering has set the standard. Many computer companies consider their products to be best. Microsoft set the old standard and Apple set the new standard. There are many social media sites that can be argued as better than others, but Facebook set the standard.

As a salesperson, I'd like you to take a moment and evaluate (or should I say self-evaluate) where you are on the standard-setting scale:

- **Are you just a rep?**

- **Are you in the top 25% of reps?**

- **Or have you achieved the status of trusted advisor who is setting standards not just in sales numbers, but also in customer loyalty, profitability, and relationships?**

What about your company? What standards is it setting? What high ethical ground has it achieved?

TAKE NOTE: Standard bearers can fall quickly. Just ask Tiger Woods.

The key word in standard setting is endure. Set standards that will last.

MAJOR CLUE: You may believe that setting the standard is out of your personal control – especially standards that your company sets. But in the new world of transparency, thanks to the Internet, mothered by Google and social media, you now have the opportunity to build your personal brand, create your personal reputation, and set your own personal standards – standards that will remain yours even if you change companies or careers.

IF YOU BREAK THE LAW: Breaking this law means you have relegated yourself to less than excellent. This might also be known as being willing to settle for "mediocre" success and lifestyle. Boy, that's a heck of a reputation: "See that guy over there? He is exceptionally mediocre!" Excellence is not just a law, it's an intention and a dedication, followed by consistent actions. If you don't demonstrate excellence, you're vulnerable to those who are one notch better.

IF YOU FOLLOW THE LAW: In my *Little Book of Leadership* you will find a full-page quote that says, "You don't just lead by example, you set the standard." This is the essence of excellence. When you demonstrate excellence, you are consistently striving to improve, rather than just resting on your laurels. Excellence is a combination of what you've done in the past, combined with what you're doing right now. Past and present determine reputation. And reputation is a report card for excellence.

CAUTION: If you fall short of excellence, don't fall into the trap of defending your position or blaming others. Take responsibility for your excellence, and rededicate yourself to both personal and business excellence.

CAUTION: There is a reality to excellence. If you believe you are excellent, and your customers or coworkers or boss do not believe you're excellent, then Buddy, you ain't excellent. Excellence is not what you believe. Rather, it's what you strive for. Excellence is what others perceive, and how they act on it and talk about it.

AHA! Excellence is achieved slowly over time.

AHA! Excellence is what your customer perceives it to be, not what you believe it to be.

AHA! Buy and read the Tom Peters and Robert Waterman book, *In Search of Excellence*, so that you can see how uncommon ordinary excellence actually is. It will give you confidence to strive to be one or two notches better than you are.

KEY TO IMPLEMENTATION: List the qualities you perceive in yourself as EXCELLENT. Then list the qualities your customer expects from you. Compare lists. Your game plan to achieve excellence is now self-evident.

If you're not setting the standard, you're fighting price. Reputation trumps price.

JEFFREY GITOMER

DELIVER VALUE FIRST

CHALLENGE

My marketing mantra for the past twenty-one years has been: *I put myself in front of people that can say yes to me, and I deliver value first.* It has been the single biggest AHA! of my entire sales and marketing career. When you ask yourself, "Which would my customers rather have, a sales pitch or something of value?" the answer becomes painfully evident. Especially if your competition is practicing it. Value first is the ultimate price-comparison weapon, and the ultimate sales-winning philosophy.

Value Is the King of Sales and the Queen of Service.

Value is perhaps the most elusive word in sales. Everyone will tell you how important it is. Very few can tell you *what* it is.

I have a distaste for the words "added value." I recommend you leave them out of your sales lexicon forever. Added value has an evil twin: "value add." Neither of which can be defined in terms of what the customer actually benefits or profits from.

Added value is usually some minor service or hard-to-define extra that the customer already expects, or takes for granted anyway. Things like same-day shipping, online ordering, parts in stock, or 24-hour service – those are not VALUE – those are A GIVEN. Those elements are expected. They are NOT incentive to buy – rather, they're just part of your business offering.

In order for you to understand the word "value" as it relates to your ability to make a sale, put the word "perceived" in front of it.

If you think it's valuable, and your customer doesn't perceive it's valuable, it ain't value.

Your customer is looking to increase THEIR sales, THEIR customer loyalty, THEIR employee loyalty, THEIR productivity, THEIR morale, THEIR profit, and to have no problems.

Are those the values you bring to the table? No? Why not? Those are the value elements that any customer would consider worthy of the word.

Your little add-on services are more of a bonus than a value.

And don't just bring them one time – consistency is the key. My secret for delivering weekly value to my customers is my weekly column and my weekly email magazine, *Sales Caffeine*.

Is value missing from your MISSION?

Most companies have a meaningless mission statement that was created by a marketing department. It's all about being number one, exceeding customer expectations, and building shareholder value. Barf.

- **What's your real mission?**

- **Is it different from your mission statement?**

- **Where's the value to the customer?**

- **Isn't that the real mission?**

What you need is a value proposition that fully explains how you help others, how they win, how you serve in terms of the customer, how that leads to loyal customers and referrals – and a mission statement that matches it.

A value proposition states what you do in terms of how a customer benefits. For example, you might say, "We provide a 4-hour service response." A "value-proposition" way of stating the same thing is, "When equipment is broken or needs repair, production stops. That's why we instituted a 4-hour or less service response. That way there is minimal loss of productivity and job profitability."

Same words, stated in terms of how the customer wins.

Value is important to a prospective customer for three reasons:

1. **It differentiates you from the competition.**

2. **It gives the customer understandable reasons to purchase.**

3. **It gives the customer the peace of mind they need to move forward. To buy.**

Value is important to an existing customer for three reasons:

1. **It builds real relationship. Relationship based on value.**

2. **It makes reorders more automatic and less bid-driven.**

3. **It eliminates competition. Most competitors thrive on "saving a customer money." NOTE: Customers don't want to save money as much as they want to produce more and make more profit.**

At the end of any sales transaction, or when an existing customer has a need, that's when "perception of value" plays its heaviest role. If the customer perceives a difference in you, and perceives a reassuring value in terms of how he or she wins, the sale is yours. If not, the sale goes to the person with the lowest price.

The more you become proficient at stating value in terms of the customer, the more it will be perceived as value by the customer.

The more you put value in terms of how they win, how they profit, and how they produce, the more it will be perceived as true value, or real value. And in the end, the value that you receive back will be the order. That's value.

Free Git ⋏ Bit...If you want to incorporate better formulated and actual value into your sales process, go to www.gitomer.com and enter the word VALUE in the GitBit box.

Show me the value, and I'll give you the sale.

JEFFREY GITOMER

What Is the Value?
Where Is the Value?
Who Perceives the Value?
Therein Lies the Sale!

THINK ABOUT THIS: You have been making value perceptions and value judgments your entire life.

You may call them decisions, moments of truth, or actions. Intuitively they focus around value – and your perception of it – or the weight you put on it as these decisions or actions are taken or made.

It's the same in sales, but in the selling process there are two values of perception and two value judgments.

One is the value perception and judgment *you* make, and the other is the value perception and judgment the *customer* makes.

Obviously, the customer's value judgment and perception rules the selling process. However, you, the salesperson, have a major impact on how the value is perceived and ultimately how their judgment is made.

Your value judgments come from:

- **How you feel about your company**
- **How you feel about your product**
- **How you feel about yourself**
- **How you feel about the customer and their buying process**

You've placed a value on yourself that reflects in your selling skills, your attitude, your belief system, your truthfulness, and your ethics. If you are willing to compromise any of those, you'll never be a successful salesperson in the long term.

That's your perspective. And then there is the customer...

Whether they're an existing customer or a prospect, they're making all kinds of value judgments about you, your product, and your company – in that order.

Much of their judgment about you is being made during the presentation itself, but in this digital age many of these perceptions and judgments are made way before you (the salesperson) enter the scene.

These days, Mother Google can create preconceived value notions that don't simply revolve around your product or your price; that's just one part of the equation. Your personal reputation and your company's reputation also play a major role in the customer's perception and judgment of value.

MAJOR UPSIDE-DOWN CLUE: Every salesperson uses Google to find more information about the company and the person they are going to meet. That same salesperson NEVER takes the same amount of time to Google themselves to see what the potential customer is finding out about them.

It's a major mystery to me why salespeople still believe they are invisible. Meanwhile, your reputation (or lack of it) is totally available to the customer long before you ever enter their office.

It will take your prospective or existing customers less than one minute to do a complete Internet search on you, and it's most likely you have never done one on yourself. Your sales hang in the balance.

WRONG THINKING: People with no internet presence, people with no brand presence, and people with little personal reputation will all make the feeble excuse that the customer is only buying price anyway. They (you) are foolishly incorrect.

If your customer is looking to make a value judgment before you arrive, what are they going to find?

NOTE WELL: If a customer is looking to make a value judgment or value perception during your presentation, much of that will occur way before the presentation takes place.

SALES REALITY: I've just given you a redefinition of the word "value" by adding the words *perceived* (perception) and *judgment*. These are the words your customer mentally uses as he or she is deciding.

Notice I have not used the words "add" or "added" when referring to the word value, nor will I ever.

I have listed the value-based elements you need to succeed. I am challenging you that you probably don't have them already. Now it's time for you to make your own value judgment whether it is worth the investment of your time to create them.

In my opinion it's not an option; it's an imperative.

Create your own value and reputation in the marketplace, so that when your prospective customer is looking for information about you, it will credibly be there.

IF YOU BREAK THE LAW: You become vulnerable to price, and you will fight price. Here is the warning sign: If you find yourself in constant price situations, it's simply because the (perceived) value of your being, your words, your actions, your reputation, your product, and/or your service offering are not evident. The challenge is to get to know what the customer considers valuable and deliver that. Customers do not want added value or value add. That says to the customer that they must buy first in order to get any value. It's an incentive, but clearly not a value.

IF YOU FOLLOW THE LAW: Big things happen when you deliver value first. The customer considers you someone that understands and is willing to help. But please, please be aware that unless the customer *perceives* you as being a person of value AND your offering as having value for them, it is of no value as it relates to the sale.

Here are a few tidbits for understanding that the customer's PERCEPTION plays a major role in the process of delivering value:

- **Perceived value is the true measure of value.**

- **Perceived value is a genuine differentiator between you and your competition.**

- **Perceived value puts you in a position where purchase is possible without respect to price.**

- **Perceived value is something that your customer is looking for when they learn about you, meet you, and throughout your entire presentation.**

- **Perceived value is something every customer considers at or near the top of their list as you try to establish and build a relationship with them.**

CAUTION: It is important to restate: if the customer does not perceive it's valuable, it ain't valuable.

AHA! Value versus incentive. Drop the words "value add" or "added value" from your sales lexicon. Here's why: if the customer has to buy something from you in order to get value, it's not really value – it's an incentive. Once you understand the difference between value and incentives, you understand value must be delivered first – in order to create the buying atmosphere and in order to create differentiation – and what you call added value or value add is merely an incentive to buy.

AHA! To best understand value, start here: take out all your literature and a red Sharpie. Circle everything your customer would consider valuable. In most cases the cap on the pen will never even come off.

AHA! The most powerful marketing principle in the world is GIVE VALUE FIRST.

AHA! Value is a customer perception.

KEY TO IMPLEMENTATION: Interview your ten best customers and ask them what they consider valuable about the company, the product(s), the service, and you. Take furious notes, look for trends and repeated elements. That's the real value. Insert that information, ideally in the form of video testimonials, into your sales presentation, and you will double your sales.

Lowest price always means lowest profit.

Value trumps price.

JEFFREY GITOMER

Unbreakable Law

COMMUNICATE IN TERMS OF THEM

CHALLENGE

Most sales presentations, most marketing messages, most brochures, most advertising, and most websites are all about the company and the product or service they offer. "We do this, we do that, we are great, we are the best." I refer to these messages as "we-we." Meanwhile the customers, you know, the ones with the money, are looking for a message about how THEY produce, how THEY win, and how THEY profit. This is a classic example of the mixed message combined with a missed message. If a customer hears a canned sales pitch that does not apply directly to them and their business, they will ask for a proposal, jerk you around as much as possible, never return your calls or messages, and buy from your competitor who was smart enough to personalize their message. Any questions? I have one: Who are your messages about?

Where's the New Customer? They're in the New World... Are You?

The customer is making a comeback – slow though it may be. And when he (or she) returns, you're going to notice a change. A big change. FAIR WARNING: How you prepare for the new customer will determine your long-term success.

REALITY: While your customers were away, online has officially taken over. It's the new showroom and the new comparison shopper. You can chat or phone in a heartbeat. You can see every option and some you never knew existed. It's fast, it's accurate, and anyone can choose anything, any time of the day or night.

Yes, the Internet has been there for a few years, but it has taken a firm hold as a trillion-dollar option for consumers and customers every place in the world. Your world.

It's a different world now. It's necessary to *revive* and *revise*. And you can be in it, or watch it pass you by.

Here are some examples of "different" on the business side. Insurance companies, car dealerships, stock brokerages, banks, homebuilders, mortgage lenders, commercial real estate agents, and residential real estate agents have all revised and restructured their business – and that's just the short list.

And the customer is different too. Way different.

Let me give you a detailed description of what the new customer (both business and consumer) looks like:

- **They're going to decide somewhat slower. They have been hesitating for more than a year.**

- **They're angry about the value of their home and their investments.**

- They will not be doing business the same way it's been done before.

- They will not be banking the same way they banked before.

- They will not be advertising the same way they advertised before.

- They will not be buying a car the same way they did before.

- They will not be buying a home the same way they did before.

- They will not be investing the same way they did before.

- They're online. Checking out your website – and your competitor's website.

- They're socializing. Telling everyone what's happening in their world and in the world.

- They're tweeting and connecting on Facebook on LinkedIn. Social media is still a firestorm.

- They're blogging about their experiences with you – for the world to read.

- They're YouTubing about their experiences with you for the world to watch – by the millions (any questions United Airlines?).

- They're Googling, not yellow-paging.

- They're texting. A lot.

- They're using their mobile device to do damn near everything.

- They're WiFi-ing in their hotel room, on the plane, in Starbucks, and at home.

- If they're reading a paper, or getting the news, it's online.

- They're as likely to watch "The Daily Show," "The Colbert Report," or listen to Howard Stern for news as they are to watch a network "news" person read a teleprompter.

- They're purchasing after midnight. By the billions.

- They're looking for ease of doing business with you.

- They are value oriented, but they will look to price as part of the decision.

- They wants a relationship.

- They want, need, and expect GREAT service after the sale.

- **They do not want to wait for anything or anyone.**

- **They need help and expert advice.**

- **They're looking for ideas and answers.**

- **They can check your price and your facts in two seconds or less on Google.**

- **They know as much about your product as you do.**

- **They know MORE about your competitor's product than you do.**

- **They can pay right now IF you can take a credit card online.**

- **They expect someone who can actually HELP to answer the phone when they call.**

- **They are SICK of off-shore call centers, erroneously called "help desks."**

- **They are SICK of you telling them how important their call is while they stand on hold.**

- **They are SICK of your recorded hold message.**

- **They demand the truth. All the time.**

- **They no longer trust the institutions they used to hold sacred.**

- **They expect you to be as computer literate as they are.**

- **They need to be understood and feel your sincere concern.**

- **While you are qualifying them, they are qualifying you.**

- **If they need a referral or recommendation, they'll go to Craigslist or Angie's List or Google or their next-door neighbor, or anyone else but you...UNLESS you have video testimonials online.**

As you're thinking about (and making excuses for) these statements, you better be thinking about your answers and responses to them too.

And you better be making the strategic decisions and game plans needed to address the new customer.

After reviewing these statements, ask yourself this BIG question: Will the new customer be *my* customer?

Beware the new customer! (They may be your old customer in disguise.)

JEFFREY GITOMER

Drill or Hole? What Are They Buying – and What Are You Selling?

A guy walks into a hardware store and says to the clerk, "I need a drill."

The clerk says, "Well, not really. You want to make a hole."

If you're in retail and your customer comes in and says, "I need a drill" or "I want a drill" or "Where are the drills?" you, the salesperson, begin some response dialogue.

REALITY: He didn't come for a drill. He needs a hole.

Now you may have heard some version of "drill-hole" in your career, but you have never heard what the situation is, how to address the buying motive, how to take control of the sale, how to gain trust, and how to create an outcome vision in the mind of the buyer.

HERE'S THE REAL LESSON: (And it can be applied to ANY sales situation when the buyer wants a service or a product and needs your help to find the right answers and achieve the required or desired outcome.) If you ask, "What kind of drill are you looking for?" you're asking an annoying, self-serving, time-wasting, price-based question. There's zero value to the customer and it's the wrong direction to go in to close a value sale.

It's likely the customer has NO IDEA what kind of drill he wants – and you, in your sales brilliance, are gonna point out the "drill aisle" and be done with it. You smile and say, "They're in the hand tool area over by the wall" or "Here's what's on sale."

NO! This is your opportunity to become an advisor rather than a traffic director. So far you don't know WHAT KIND OF HOLE THE CUSTOMER NEEDS.

- **How big (what diameter) of a hole are you drilling?**
- **What kind of material are you drilling into?**
- **How deep is the hole?**
- **Are you drilling indoors or outdoors?**

If you're trying to show the customer the 3/8-inch drill "on sale" and the customer needs a 1/2-inch hole, you're gonna have an unhappy customer. But if you know it's a 1/2-inch hole through a wooden post, you can recommend the right drill and also tell them they need a "starter hole" with a smaller drill bit to ensure a perfect outcome.

Okay, you get it! Drill – hole – want – need – outcome.

But Jeffrey, you whine, how does this apply to me and my sales?

Well, it applies to all sales that every salesperson makes – including yours:

- **I need a filling in my tooth. No, you want to be healthy and pain free.**
- **I need copies. No, you want to send a full-color proposal that reflects your image and wins the sale.**
- **I need a new roof. No, you want to have no leaks and enjoy quality of life.**
- **I need a credit card. No, you don't have cash or you don't want to spend your cash.**
- **I need tickets to a concert. No, your favorite group of all time is playing and you have never seen them before. It's on your bucket list!**
- **I need to find a restaurant. No, you need to eat in a restaurant that serves food quickly.**
- **I need new tires. No, you want to be safe on the road whether you're traveling alone or with your family.**
- **I need a flight to New York City. No, you need to attend a business conference or you're taking a once-in-a-lifetime trip with your family.**

HERE'S THE REALITY: The buyer, the prospect, and the customer expect you to have knowledge of their stuff, not just your stuff. For the message to be transferable, they need to feel your passion, your belief, your knowledge, your ideas, and your sincerity beyond the hype of the sales pitch.

- **You have to know their industry – not just your product.**
- **You have to know their business – not just your product.**
- **You have to know what's new and what's next – not just your product.**

- **You have to know the trends – not just your product.**
- **You have to know their marketing – not just your product.**
- **You have to know their productivity – not just your product.**
- **You have to know their profit – not just your product.**

NOTE WELL: Just because you don't have what the customer needs, doesn't mean they no longer need it.

If I call a hotel to book a room and they say, "Sorry, we're full," I respond, "Oh, I guess I don't need a room after all."

Think past sale to *genuine need* and *desired outcome.*

What does the customer need or want to do *after* the sale is made? How can you show her or prove to her you have the answers and you are the best choice to create a happy ending – the ultimate outcome?

That's what the customer is really buying: OUTCOME.

- **It's not just what it is (a perceived need) – a drill.**
- **It's not just what it does – makes a hole.**
- **It's the desired outcome – the result of drilling the hole.**

If you're looking to successfully sell at your price, build a relationship, and earn a referral you better stop selling the features and benefits of your product, and look to what happens after the sale – after the customer takes ownership.

If you're able to find (by uncovering and asking for) the desired outcome and agree that your answer, your solution, or your idea will be the best one – the customer will buy.

IF YOU BREAK THE LAW: About now, you're getting the message that the customer expects stuff about them, not stuff about you. Your brochure will fit conveniently in a shredder if it's all about you. And your presentation will get shredded if it's all about you. We-we presentations break "the law of them" in a way that is certain to be either ignored or price-based. The expensive part of breaking this law is that it will transcend to EVERY presentation you make until you fix it. This is not just a one-time loss, it's an all-of-the-time loss. The good news is it's fixable if you apply "the law of value" and the "law of customization" to ALL your messages and presentations. Apply value and customization to all of your messages, and almost by magic, we-we turns into them-them. And them-them turns into sales.

IF YOU FOLLOW THE LAW: When you begin your presentation with an idea in favor of the customer, or a question that shows you've prepared, or statement of fact that impacts the customer's business, you will immediately notice that the customer is paying solid attention to you and your words. You'll notice that the presentation is both well received and respected. You'll notice that the customer is asking questions about delivery and ownership. And most important, you will notice that your level of confidence when you're presenting is transferable because it has both value and personalization.

AHA! Evaluate your company's literature for value TO the customer. Evaluate your slides and presentation for value and customization IN FAVOR of the customer.

Making the transition from me-me and we-we, to you-you and them-them is NOT an option.

KEY TO IMPLEMENTATION: The customer becomes interested in you when he or she knows you're interested in them. Partial proof is that you come into the meeting totally prepared. Not just with information pertaining to the customer and how they win and how they profit. You must also offer undeniable final proof to lower the final barrier. Video testimonials from others who have purchased based on your message and are willing to give testimony as to your validity are final proof.

11

ASK BEFORE YOU TELL

CHALLENGE

Questions are the heart of the sale. Questions convert "selling" to "buying." Questions uncover facts, needs, motives, emotions, and will lead you to a sale 100 times faster than making your presentation. Knowing this, you'd assume that all salespeople would ask brilliant questions. And you would be wrong.

SIMPLE TRUTH: If you don't ask amazing, emotionally engaging questions, you will lose to a competitor who does.

A New Way to Look at Questions and Engagement: Emotionally.

When you're asking an existing or prospective customer a question, the object is to get them to think and respond emotionally.

To most salespeople this strategy sounds like a foreign language.

START YOUR THINKING HERE: The sale is made emotionally and justified logically. Once you understand that fact, it makes perfect sense to engage the customer emotionally to set the tone for them to decide to buy.

Most salespeople are taught the difference between open-ended and closed-ended questions. A closed-ended question is one that results in a yes or no answer. An open-ended question is one that begins to create dialogue with the customer. Open-ended questions are good, but they don't necessarily ellicit emotion. This process is necessary to understand, but at its core it is passé.

Here's a new way of thinking about your questioning strategy: logic-based questions vs. emotion-based questions.

This thought process and strategy will give you a new awareness about how customers think and decide. And by using emotion-based questions, you can get them to decide on you.

CAUTION AND CHALLENGE: This is insight to a new questioning process that will help you formulate emotionally engaging questions. I'll give you phrases to use, and a few sample questions. Your job is to understand the process and create your own questions based on your product, service, customer needs, and customer's desired outcome. Questions that draw out their emotion, and keep focus away from logic – AKA price.

Logic-based questions center around old-world "qualifying" questions. These are questions that both annoy and aggravate the customer. Logic-based questions basically ask for money information so the salesperson can begin to salivate. "What's your present payment?" or "What have you paid in the past?" or "What's your budget?" or "Do you want to lease or buy?" These questions fall under the category of "none of your business."

KEY CONCEPT: Do not qualify the buyer, let them qualify themselves because you're so friendly, engaging, and genuinely interested.

The late, great Dale Carnegie said, "You can make more friends in two months by becoming really interested in other people, than you can in two years by trying to get other people interested in you."

Emotion-based questions ask about the customer's life, not their money. Prior to beginning your "presentation," ask the customer emotion-based questions that begin with the words, "How long have you been thinking about..." or "What were you hoping for..."

Get the customer to paint their vision of outcome. Get the customer to paint their picture of "after they buy."

Emotion-based questions draw out feelings – feelings that will lead to true engagement and honest answers about how your product or service will affect their expected outcome.

During the sales presentation, ask emotion-based questions such as:

- **"Is this what you had in mind?"**

- **"How do you see this serving your purpose?"**

- **"How do you see your family enjoying this?"**

Or take it even deeper with:

- **"What do you think Bobby will say when he sees this?"**

- **"What are you hoping to achieve?"**

- **"How will you use this in your business?"**

- **"How do you envision this will add to your productivity?"**

- **"How do you believe this will affect your profit?"**

MAJOR POINT OF UNDERSTANDING: People don't actually come to purchase. They come to purchase because they want to USE. What happens AFTER the purchase is way more important to the customer than the actual purchasing process. Drawing out their emotion during the process is the key to getting them to take ownership.

Whether you are selling to a consumer or a business, whether you are selling on the phone or face-to-face, the process and the emotional involvement are the same.

Someone wants to take ownership, and your job is to get them to visualize it, be engaged by you, agree with you, believe you, have confidence in you, trust you, accept your price, and pull the trigger.

The key to this is emotional involvement.

No manipulation, no pressure, no old-world sales techniques, no neuro-linguistic programming. Just friendly and genuine emotional engagement that touches the heart and the mind simultaneously.

"Jeffrey, I've been taught to 'find the pain.' Is that emotional?" Yes, but in a negative way. A very negative way. Pain is a negative emotion – or as I call it, a "none-of-your-business emotion." Dumb questions like, "What keeps you up at night?" create an uneasy, uncomfortable atmosphere between you and the customer. And most of the time, if you're asking a negative-based question, the customer will not give you a real answer.

Don't find the pain. Find the pleasure.

Pleasure evokes positive emotion. "Tell me about your vacation." "How is Morgan following your passion for fashion?" "How is Henry inspired by your love of golf?" "Where was your biking trip this year?"

- **Find their pleasure.**
- **Find their purpose.**
- **Find their expected outcome.**
- **Uncover their true emotional motives.**

...And you will find their wallet. Now that's pleasure.

When you can get the customer to visualize outcome, you also have them visualizing ownership – otherwise known to you as "purchase."

JEFFREY GITOMER

What Keeps Me Up at Night?
None of Your Business!

Salespeople (not you of course) are known for asking poor questions –
questions that are not only embarrassing, questions that are also rude.
And I would be remiss if I didn't add: questions that make them appear
desperate and pressing for a sale.

The dumbest question in sales is "What will it take to get your business?"
It's by far the *worst* question you can ask a customer. It makes you a price
seller rather than a value provider, and it makes you look like you "need"
the sale rather than want to earn and grow a relationship.

REALITY: There is a close second to the dumbest. It's "What keeps you up
at night?"

Are you kidding me? NONE OF YOUR BUSINESS, that's what!

You're at the beginning of a sales call, trying to build positive rapport
and earn some level of "like" and "trust," and you're asking me that kind
of question? It's almost as dumb as trying to "find the pain." Please don't
get me started on 1972 sales manipulation and insincerity.

Why not ask the prospect a question that relates to their real life and
their present situation that's potentially more revealing than a Miss
America question?

MAJOR AHA! QUESTION: *What wakes you up in the morning?*

It's a positive-based question that, when asked with a smile, will get
you real answers, real facts, and reveal real truths. It's lighthearted, but
powerful, and when followed up with "what else" or "then what" will
create a dialogue that is totally customer focused – thereby achieving
the purpose of the interaction.

HERE'S WHAT TO DO: Think of all the answers on the next page IN TERMS
OF YOURSELF, FIRST. What wakes YOU up? It reveals your top-of-mind
thoughts, issues, concerns, goals, problems, and attitude toward them.
Got it? Now direct them at the customer or prospect and listen to the
eye-popping, ear de-waxing, and self-qualifying answers.

You ask, "What wakes you up in the morning?" They answer:

- **Light of day.** Easy answer. Leads to, "Then what?"

- **Alarm clock.** Another easy answer. Still leads to, "Then what?"

- **Kids.** Great answer! Leads to all kinds of mutual discussion points and common interests if you also have kids.

- **Relationships.** A bit touchy. Let the prospect lead.

- **Coffee – shower – exercise – the news.** These subjects might reveal things you share in common.

- **The day and things to be done.** People will make their day more important than your day. And you'll feel it when they chatter and complain about "having so much to do."

Now let's take it deeper. Asking the "then what?" question will get them to the next phase of their reality. It started out light; now it gets to some real issues. You might ask, "What else wakes you up?" They might say:

- **Money, or the lack of it.** Think of this one in terms of yourself. Go lightly, but it's very revealing.

- **Health issues.** A physical ailment or medical condition may impact their attention span or decision-making capability.

- **Pain.** If they're in pain, then the pain will affect concentration and span of attention.

- **Energy/positive anticipation.** This is GREAT. An enthusiastic person can connect with your compelling presentation and catch your positive feelings.

- **All the stuff he or she is excited about.** These are golden issues that need to be embellished on and compared to what it will be like when your stuff gets its chance.

- **Big issues.** IRS, business failure, damaged reputation, lawsuits. A pending merger or pending big order could be a positive sign.

- **Business issues.** The day-to-day often gets in the way of the month-to-month and the year-to-year. Stay away from the mundane, and be aware of the complainer.

- **Personal issues.** Family and relationship issues can have a real impact (either way) on your meeting outcome – pending marriage or pending divorce?

- **Career issues.** Work, boss, sales, people, and events can have huge implications on your need to do something today.

- **Nagging issues (worries).** These are elements that slow down the actions a customer is willing to take. If you know what they are, you'll be less likely to be impatient, and more likely to create a winning plan to make the sale.

- **Unfinished issues.** Stuff undone. "Wait until after..." are defeating words to the ears of salespeople. But if you know what the issues are, you can get a better sense of "when."

- **Projects underway.** Most people are limited in the amount of work and projects they can take on. When your customer dwells on "present situation" and "major project" you can expect postponement. Make sure you nail down expected completion date.

- **Deadlines.** If it's close, you're toast. Best thing is to offer assistace.

MAJOR CLUE: Don't overdo the process. Ask a few questions, gain a few answers, and move on. As a result, you will then have some new information, maybe some common interests, a few smiles, and certainly a prospect who is engaged and thinking.

I made you think, didn't I? You can do the same with your prospect. Stay away from defensive-based questions. Your responses will lead you down the right path – the business relationship and mutual respect path.

IF YOU BREAK THE LAW: When you fully understand my personal law, "People don't like to be sold, but they love to buy," you immediately see that asking your way to the sale is much more powerful than telling your way to the sale. You have broken the law if you do not start with questions. You have broken the law if questions are not in the middle of your presentation. You have broken the law if you do not end your presentation with questions. Powerful, emotionally engaging questions.

NOTE WELL: If you feel you ask a lot of questions, and still are not getting the results you're looking for, then it's likely that your questions are old-world "qualifying" questions – logic-based questions based on money and your need, or should I say your greed, to make the sale.

IF YOU FOLLOW THE LAW: This law is based on power. Power in preparation, power in the question itself, and power in your ability to ask the question in a way that the customer is impressed with your knowledge, impressed with your preparation, and forced to answer in a way that benefits you. Superior questions create superior engagement. Emotional questions create emotional engagement. Both of these elements create winning scenarios that result both in sales and relationships. When the customer is impressed by the quality of your questions, they will be more willing and more forthcoming to provide truthful information.

BONUS: By following this law you will continue to gain expertise, and even sales supremacy, as you face customers who are increasingly demanding and wanting to know "what's in it for them."

CAUTION: Please don't think that one or two questions will take you to the Promised Land. More like twenty or twenty-five questions are what you need as a foundation to build true engagement and respect.

AHA! Formulating powerful, engaging questions takes more work than you realize. Allocate and dedicate time to make this happen.

AHA! The ultimate engagement question makes the customer stop and think, consider new information, and respond in terms of you.

AHA! Telling is selling. Asking is buying. Asking is listening, learning, and discovering the customer's motive or motives to buy. You cannot make sales at your price without them.

KEY TO IMPLEMENTATION: Collaboration is the key to gaining question dominance. Start with ten of your customers. Talk to them one-by-one. Ask them why they bought, why they love you, why they remain loyal, how much price plays a factor in your relationship, why they would refer you, and their experience with your product or service. Record all of the conversations. From those notes you will be able to formulate powerful questions based on the content of their answers. Once these questions have been formulated, meet with your coworkers, your boss, and your CEO. Present your questions and ask for their insight, their feedback, and their ideas. This collaboration will lead you to the power questions you need for engagement, respect, impact, and sales.

The ultimate power question makes the customer understand that you're there for both business and value.

JEFFREY GITOMER

12

SERVE MEMORABLY

CHALLENGE

Think about the most memorable service you have ever received. Ever tell anyone about it? Now think about the service you provide to your customers. How many people are talking about you? ANSWER: Not enough. Memorable service cannot be a haphazard or once-in-a-while thing. It has to be on purpose. It's as much a game plan as marketing, advertising, or social media.

To Serve Is to Rule.
Who Are You Ruling?

You have heard stories of great service. Nordstrom, Lexus, AutoZone, Les Schwab, Zappos, and individuals in small businesses that have gone WAY BEYOND the norm to provide extraordinary service.

You have probably heard them enough to make you sick. Especially if your service is lousy.

At the airport you see a huge banner of an airline BRAGGING about the "satisfaction award" they just won from J.D. Power.

HUH? Am I missing something? When did an airline deserve to win anything? Maybe the luggage fee award, but I can't see how anyone who makes a customer wait endlessly on the phone, get dinged for everything under the sun, be penalized to change a ticket, and stand on line for an hour to receive "service" – just to get a boarding pass and get charged for a bag or two – should be rewarded. Please help me to understand the "award" part of that.

But I digress.

It's time to wake up and realize things ain't what they used to be. And in spite of what you may hear or read from some economic or government genius, it will be a long time until things return to the way they used to be (if they ever do).

Meanwhile in the real world, you and I have a job to do, a business to run, customers to serve and people to employ, and attitudes (morale) to maintain. Some will take these tasks more seriously than others.

So now is not the time to point fingers and blame. Now is the time to take responsibility – personal responsibility – for the outcome of business success, especially your business success. Whether you own it, sell for it, work in it, or are part of the family of someone employed, NOW IS THE TIME.

REALITY: There is no handout, er, I mean bailout coming in the mail for you. The check is NOT in the mail.

REALITY: You are the bailout. I am the bailout. Together we are the collective bailout.

REALITY: Your victory starts with your customer's victory. Without customers, there is no chance of winning.

REALITY: There are fewer customers, and those that are left have less to spend.

NOTE: I didn't say, "nothing to spend," I said, "less to spend."

Now is the time to think: service before sales

Here are the elements of your bailout, your survival, your sales, and your success:

- **Success starts with attitude training.** If you or your coworkers are angry, afraid, or resentful, it will reflect in the way customers are served.

- **It costs nothing extra to be friendly.** But friendly is worth a fortune, and a reputation.

- **Identify every service opportunity.** There are probably less than twenty-five actual opportunities to serve coworkers and customers. Once you identify them, have a company meeting (or meetings) to identify best practices – and dates to IMPLEMENT new and better service strategies and expressions.

- **Service is an individual not a company.** Serve for yourself first. This is perhaps the most difficult of all the points I'm making. It means you have to be personally responsible for everything you say and do – for yourself and for others.

GREAT NEWS! If you start today, you'll be just in time to catch the wave of customers as the economy begins to tick up – or should I say uptick? Either way, the clock is running. Better catch it before it blows by you – to your competition.

Service is being kind, having a heart, and doing the right thing – the best thing – in favor of your customers.

JEFFREY GITOMER

Service Leads to Sales, If You Know How to Act and How to Ask.

Every time a customer calls it's an opportunity. The only question is: how are you taking advantage of it?

Don't answer with a "thank you for the call," telling me how important my call is while you put me on hold for the next available agent. Or to "serve me better," ask me to select from among the following eight options.

Selecting from among the following eight options is not one of MY options – and I have the money – and you want the money – and you need the money – so wise up.

The last things employers should cut are sales, service, and training. The FIRST thing to cut is executive pay, then management pay, then eliminate middle management as needed. OR MAKE THEM SALESPEOPLE, and have them contribute to the effort.

Meanwhile, customers need help, service, and answers. Your ability to help them in a timely manner, and serve them memorably, determines your reputation and your fate.

Here's how to serve:

- **Start friendly NO MATTER how they act or talk.**
- **Don't worry about how you feel. Worry about how they feel.**
- **Ask them how you can help them the most.**
- **Don't tell them what you can't do. Tell them what you can do.**
- **Get them to see that the solution you offer, or answer they need, is the one they are expecting, and the one they are pleased with.**
- **Engage them personally during the conversation.**
- **Make CERTAIN customers are happy as a result of the call.**
- **Follow through on your promises with action and communication.**

Here's the secret to service success:

- **Keep it short, but get the info you need to help them.**

- **If the customer is angry, keep it real short, but arrange a second call after the complaint is resolved. Tell them what will happen in their favor, and tell them fast.**

Follow up with the unexpected to set up a sale. I refer to it as PLUS ONE:

- **Email thanks. Tell them how much you enjoyed talking to them and how much you appreciate their business.**

- **Email them back with your ideas or suggestions.**

- **Email them back with a solution, or your promise to repair.**

- **Have a salesperson call after the situation was resolved.**

CUSTOMER REALITY:

- **I don't want to wait on the phone.**

- **I especially don't want to listen to your self-serving messages as I wait.**

- **I don't want to stand on line.**

- **I don't want to be told no.**

- **I don't want excuses about why you can't.**

- **I don't want to hear about your policy.**

- **I don't want to donate to your charities.**

- **I want help, I want YES, and I want it fast.**

ECONOMIC REALITY:

- **When business is down, it's likely morale is down. Invest in attitude training for every member of the team FIRST.**

- **When business is down, the best way to get more sales is by creating more friendly, human interaction.**

- **When business is down, the best way to gain loyalty from existing customers, and get more sales (the surest path to survival and growth), is by making service IMPROVEMENTS, not service cuts.**

Okay, so now that you know what to do, what are you going to DO about it? What actions are you willing to take? What investment are you willing to make? Do you understand it's ALL about customer loyalty (not customer satisfaction)?

MAJOR CLUE: Keep in mind that no company ever CUT their way to success.

REALITY: You cut your way to safety. You have to SELL your way to success.

If you want to win in this or any economy, you must be ready to win – ready with the right attitude, the right information, and the right service heart.

How ready are you?

IF YOU BREAK THE LAW: If a computer answers your phone, you have broken the law. If you use the word "policy," you have broken the law. Start there. The penalty for breaking this law is two-fold. Loss of reputation AND loss of customer. There are very few laws that have a higher penalty, and very few laws that are EASIER to fix. You don't have to worry about monitoring your bad service. Your customers will do it for you, on Facebook and on Twitter. Your job is to fix it and continually improve it.

IF YOU FOLLOW THE LAW: Your business reputation, both online and person-to-person, will soar! You'll become known for taking ordinary daily business actions and turning them into pleasant customer surprises. The result is not just more business – it's more loyal customers, more referrals, greater reputation, and more profit. Think about that the next time you ask me to "select from among the following eight options."

CAUTION: Ordinary, even polite, service is unacceptable. It will not give you the competitive edge or the business advantage that memorable service will.

At the end of any transaction, that's when the customer STARTS talking about you. They will say one of five things about what transpired: something great, something good, nothing, something bad, or something real bad. And whatever they say leads to the next sale – either at your place, or your competition's place.

The cool part is: you choose.

AHA! My "memorable mantra": Find something personal; do something memorable.

AHA! Grow from good, to great, to memorable.

KEY TO IMPLEMENTATION: Start with smart, happy people. Then define what is memorable and how everyone can achieve memorability with daily interactions (Southwest Airlines does it with friendly people and humor). Meet with all senior people and staff to create the ideas that wow, and gain the permission to wow at the same time. Then train AND empower everyone with specific phrases and actions they can take on behalf of customers.

Unbreakable Law

13

EXCHANGE LOYALTY

CHALLENGE

My 1998 benchmark book, *Customer Satisfaction Is Worthless, Customer Loyalty Is Priceless*, still serves as the standard for defining the difference between "satisfied" and "loyal." Are your customers satisfied, or very satisfied, and still doing some business with your competitor? Stop fooling yourself. The question you have to ask yourself is, are my customers LOYAL? One notch below satisfaction is dissatisfaction, or anger, or worse. In fact, you have plenty of customers that are never satisfied, but still continue to do business with you. What are those customers called? They're called loyal!

What's Your Proactive Marketing Approach to Loyalty?

I just received this email:

Dear Jeffrey, I am a huge fan. I recently had a WOW experience that completely coincides with your philosophy on customer loyalty versus satisfaction. Today, I received the following email from Amazon:

> Hello, We noticed that you experienced poor video playback while watching the following rental on Amazon Video On Demand: The Hunger Games. We're sorry for the inconvenience and have issued you a refund for the following amount: $3.99. While Amazon Video On Demand transactions are typically not refundable, we are happy to make an exception in this case. This refund should be processed within the next 2 to 3 business days and will appear on your next billing statement for the same credit card used to purchase this item

This is amazing to me for a few reasons. Yes, I did notice that my movie was buffering more than usual and, yes, it was annoying. However, it was nothing more than a minor frustration. I didn't complain. I didn't complete a survey or give any feedback about this experience. Truthfully, until I received this email, I hadn't given it a second thought.

When I got this email, it stopped me in my tracks. THEY NOTICED. They noticed that this particular experience was below their normal standards. But what's more important, THEY NOTICED WITHOUT ME TELLING THEM.

Good companies would refund my money if I complained. Of course they would; that is expected. I never have had a company refund my money without being prompted. Never. And this, this was a surprise.

Would I have used them again even if they had not refunded my money? Yes, often. So what's the difference? I wouldn't have REFERRED them. I received this email today at 2:18 pm. Since then, I told all my coworkers, posted this on my Facebook wall, and now am writing you.

Amazon lost four dollars today, but they gained a customer for life! It was so impressive, I had to share. Make it a great day, Candace

Brilliant, eh? Proactive, memorable service.

Amazon is monitoring the quality of their streaming bandwidth and can identify quality issues. Then, they DO SOMETHING ABOUT IT. No waste-of-time-and-money "survey," no phony empty apology, just a good, old-fashioned admission of guilt and a proactive refund for poor performance.

My bet is Amazon has given thousands of these, and the same customer response has happened with every one of them. What a strategy! Let's make sure the customer's experience was great, or let's give them a refund.

Simple. Powerful. Profitable. Give up $4.00 to earn thousands. I wonder who thought that one up? Certainly not their advertising agency.

Look at the elements of business and sales as a result of Amazon's action and customer reaction: a huge WOW, several social postings, an amazing testimonial, customer loyalty, and pass-along value that cannot be measured on any ROI scale. Amazon's actions cultivate return on proactive, memorable service – the WOW factor, social response, and customer word-of-mouth. It's WAY beyond "priceless" – in the long term, it's worth a fortune.

HERE'S YOUR LESSON: You can invest in some marketing program to reach new people – or you can invest in giving your existing customers the best service possible, and let THEM find new people for you.

PREDICTION: I'll bet the investment in existing customer experience is one-tenth the cost of any marketing program. In fact, I doubt this type of outreach is even on a marketing team's mindset. They're still in the Stone Age measuring ROI.

Amazon has led the Internet all the way with vision and tenacity. Quality and value. Ease of doing business and buy with one click. Purchase suggestions and published reviews. Not just price – delivery.

And now add to that list: proactive WOW interaction. They dominate because they differentiate. They dominate because they innovate. They don't study the market – they create it.

Take this lesson to heart – and take it to your customers. If you come up with something creatively compelling, you can also take it to the bank!

Proactive service isn't priceless. You can bank it.

JEFFREY GITOMER

Customer Wellness…the Best Way to Prevent Ill Customers.

Everyone is talking about the rising cost of health care. Not me. I'm talking about the health and well-being of your customers.

- **How healthy is their relationship with you?**

- **What's your cost of keeping them healthy?**

- **Is it on the rise?**

Let me give you a clue about the cost of customer health: it pales in comparison to the cost of losing customers.

- **Have any customers that are in poor health?**

- **Have any customers who are sick (of dealing with you)?**

- **Have any customers dying to replace you?**

What's the cost of that?

If your customer is angry – think of them as having a business illness. They're deathly sick of you! And like human illness, business illness has various stages of debility. Once discovered, you will go to all lengths, and spend thousands of fruitless dollars, to try to save the patient.

But if the illness is discovered too late, the patient is likely to die.

You could have spent far fewer dollars and prevented this illness from occurring. Instead of waiting until your customer is terminally ill, why not institute a customer wellness program to prevent illness from occurring in the first place?

Hey, wait a minute. That sounds too easy!

HERE'S A WAKE UP CALL: Prevention is the best way, the easiest way, and the least expensive way. It's also the competition-prevention way.

Here is my 12.5 step wellness program – a success formula for you and your coworkers to serve memorably and keep customers loyal:

1. Establish benchmarks. Minimum acceptable standards, methods of response, decision parameters, a list of every reason a customer calls, a list of every customer complaint, a list of every customer expectation, and a documented "best response" to each of those situations.

2. Be empowered with specific actions to take based on your benchmarks. Everyone on the team should be empowered to say yes. Leave the empowerment to say no to senior management.

3. Start with "YES!" Everyone needs to start with attitude training FIRST. Get there by whatever positive means it takes.

4. Ongoing training is key. Start with YES! Attitude and then develop fundamental skills in achieving goals, understanding yourself and your coworkers, enhancing pride, accepting responsibility, listening to understand, effective communication, embracing change, making decisions, memorable service, and working as a team.

5. Develop a standardized "yrlpe response" formula. Be sure everyone on the team knows how to execute it perfectly.

6. Ask your customers how you can serve them better. Listen to discover what your customer values most in a relationship with you. Ask them where you can improve. Ask them to evaluate your strengths and weaknesses in those areas of prime importance to them. Find out their perceptions and make them yours. Modify or change your approach and perceptions to meet theirs.

7. Evaluate your own strengths and weaknesses. Make a plan for *weakness improvement* that has a deadline and measurable results.

8. Identify your competitive advantages (your super strengths). Play to those as often as possible. To identify them, ask customers.

9. Stay in front of your customer. More than your competition. Develop tools that aid that process (email magazine, social media presence).

10. Serve exceptionally and memorably every time you encounter a customer. Treat every customer as if they were a celebrity.

11. Surprise your customers as often as you can. Exceed their expectations in a memorable way. You know what it feels like when you are surprised. Do it to someone else. Get people talking about you.

12. Decide you are willing to go the extra mile. Sometimes extra effort is required to make service happen. You have to have a willingness to go the extra mile to achieve it.

12.5 Your report card is unsolicited referrals. Unsolicited referrals are the measurement of your success, the testament of your quality, and the report card of your ability to serve.

Think you can do it? Think you and everyone in your company can make customer wellness happen? Want my opinion? You have no choice.

Wellness and health care are two of the biggest issues in America. Make the wellness of your customers *your* biggest issue.

Free Git X Bit...If you want the formula for ongoing customer loyalty, go to www.gitomer.com and enter the word LOYALTY in the GitBit box.

IF YOU BREAK THE LAW: Failure to exchange loyalty means that every one of your customers is vulnerable to your competition. And not just vulnerable for price. Vulnerable for service. Vulnerable for friendliness. And vulnerable for perceived value. Without loyalty you begin blaming everything and everyone, rather than taking responsibility for your actions and your responses. Think about this as it relates to your business... How much does it cost to acquire a new customer? Why would you jeopardize losing that customer because of poor service? Investing in memorable service and keeping customers loyal pays more dividends than investing in new customer acquisition.

IF YOU FOLLOW THE LAW: Customer loyalty is the highest measurement of business success. That customer will do business with you for years, they will fight before they switch, and they will proactively tell other people how great you are. Loyal customers provide the base of financial security for a company. They are more profitable per sale, they are easier to do business with per transaction, and they are likely to be your advocate on social media. There is no measurement for customer loyalty other than a reorder and a referral, but there is measurement in increased profitability and increased reputation.

CAUTION: If you believe you have a GREAT relationship with a B2B customer, and you still have to bid or quote to get an order, rethink that belief. You have a bidding relationship. They ain't loyal.

CAUTION: Please do not confuse customer loyalty with forced loyalty. Airline miles are forced loyalty. Companies refer to loyalty programs, but in reality they're incentive programs. They have nothing to do with customer loyalty.

Customer satisfaction is the LOWEST LEVEL of acceptable service.

AHA! Most big companies claim to have a 97% satisfaction rate, and yet post a 15% lost customer rate. HUH? Bogus measurements create false understanding and loss of internal belief. (And by the way, the 3% of customers that are not satisfied are telling hundreds, maybe thousands, of people on social media.)

AHA! Actions that create loyal customers: Friendly people who answer the phone on the second ring or less. Immediate response to service issues. Recovery from service issues in a memorable way. Never using the word "policy." Never arguing with a customer. Never hanging up on a customer. Never being discourteous to a customer.

KEY TO IMPLEMENTATION: Jump into reality mode. *Begin measuring two things about your existing customer base:*

1. **Will they do business with you again?**
2. **Will they refer someone to you proactively?**

No other measurement has an ounce of credibility. No other measurement has a penny's worth of value.

In order to make this law a reality in your business, you must get rid of the word "satisfaction" from your lexicon and stop trying to pat yourself on the head with bogus statistics.

If your customers are healthy, you become wealthy.

JEFFREY GITOMER

Unbreakable Law

EARN TRUST

CHALLENGE

Trust is the fulcrum point of your life's success. Who do you trust? Who trusts you? Tough questions. Maybe the toughest ever. With one exception: do you trust yourself? You may give a knee-jerk YES to that question, but upon closer inspection the answer may not be that definitive. And even more interesting, you can't/won't trust others until you trust yourself. Trust comes from within. And if you're shaky about yourself, it will be obvious to others, and as a result, you won't be as trustable – or trust attractive. My *Little Teal Book of Trust* provides a much more in-depth look at trust. The goal is to get you on the path to trust yourself, trust others, and become trustworthy.

CAUTION: Read carefully. Admit and confront your shortcomings, your fears, your trepidations, your past trust experiences, and implement each trust element individually and carefully.

Mutual Trust.
The Essence of an Ideal
Relationship.

In the 1950s, Johnny Carson got his television start hosting a show called, "Who Do You Trust?"

The premise of the show was accepting or challenging the answers given by your partner. Did you trust the answers or did you doubt the answers?

Much the same in your life. Much the same in your sales. Much the same in your relationships.

If I ask you who you trust, it requires deep thought.

A few people you can name in a heartbeat, but as your thinking deepens, a lot of consideration comes into play before you actually name someone.

I wonder who trusts you.

THINK ABOUT THIS: Would your customers think of you immediately as someone they trust, or is there a hesitation and a lot of consideration before they name you? (If at all.)

People are always asking me how to build trust. The answer is quite simple. Use a process of self-discovery:

- **Make a list of people you trust. List why you trust them. Upon review of the list, you will at once understand how to gain the trust of others. Quality performance? Quality advice? A history of truth? NOTE: Those you trust have EARNED trust over time. So must you.**

- **Make a list of the people who you are CERTAIN trust you. Why do they trust you? List the trustworthy characteristics you possess and you'll have an even greater understanding how you give trust *and* how to earn it.**

Trust begins with the truth. Trust ends with the truth. And in between the words you speak and the actions you take determine the level of trust you can achieve.

NOTE WELL: Words and actions are not the only elements by which trust is achieved. There are subtleties in your personality that can build trust or tear it down. They're called characteristics.

How you speak, for example, can add to or subtract from your ability to be trusted. And the consistency of your actions, not just the actions themselves, can go a long way toward building trust.

Your reliability, your punctuality, your enthusiasm, your humor, your honesty, your sincerity, your social presence, your method of dress, and your reputation all play a role in building trust with others.

I have found that consistent, positive, helpful actions and exposure over an extended period of time have helped me build major trust with my employees, my customers, and my community.

I have also found that consistent writing and the publishing of my thoughts help me build attraction with prospective customers and at the same time keep my loyal customers engaged and responsive.

And so can you.

MAJOR POINT OF UNDERSTANDING: If you're with me, and I like you, there is a POSSIBILITY I can trust you. In the middle of like and trust, I must believe you and have confidence in you.

I have to perceive a difference in you from the others, and I have to perceive a value in you and your product or service beyond your price.

The key to selling is trust, but the key to trust is "like." That's it.

Trust leads to sales.

Free Git Bit... Want the 21.5 Elements of Trust from my *Little Teal Book of Trust*? Go to www.gitomer.com and enter the words ELEMENTS OF TRUST in the GitBit box.

Learning Trust from the Dark Side.

Everyone wants to be fully trusted. The reality is very few people are. Most of the time lack of trust isn't from failure to gain trust, it's from the fact there was some degree of trust, but by your (their) words, actions, or deeds – it became lost.

Sales CANNOT be made without trust.

When you can identify what does and does not make you trustworthy and admit your shortcomings, you can become trustworthy again.

Self-discovery can help bring your trustworthiness back.

Self-discovery leads to personal recovery.

Ask yourself...

- **Who have I lost trust in? Make a list.**
- **Why did you lose it? Write the reasons down.**
- **Who has lost trust in me? Make a list.**
- **Why did they lose it? Write the reasons down.**

Here are a few helpful "lost trust" hints:

- **Did you lie?**
- **Were you often late?**
- **Were you unreliable?**
- **Did you have unfulfilled or unmet promises?**
- **Did you perform poorly?**

To climb back up the trust ladder requires BOTH learning and doing. But always keep in mind trust is NOT asked for. Trust is EARNED.

Here are 4.5 things you can do to build trust – keeping in mind that trust is gained slowly over time:

1. **Find and read Napoleon Hill's legendary *Law of Reciprocity*. It states that "you get what you give."**

2. **Risk giving trust – especially first.**

3. **Be vulnerable when you give trust.**

4. **Be honored when you receive trust.**

4.5 **Know that the path to keeping continuing trust is truth and consistent, trustworthy actions.**

IF YOU BREAK THE LAW: It's not good to lose the trust... of anyone. And the interesting part of losing it is how fast it happens. Especially compared to how long it took to build it.

The penalties for breaking this law are very difficult to propose, describe, or predict. But in most cases, there's both a monetary cost and a personal cost.

If you lose the trust of a customer, you'll eventually lose the customer. And it's most likely that your reputation will suffer as well.

It's the same with a friend or spouse. There are several actions that cause loss of trust, but the main two are failure to speak the truth and failure to act ethically. These two elements should never be violated, yet they are, and all too frequently.

IF YOU FOLLOW THE LAW: If you have earned trust, it's because your consistent actions over time have both reduced the risk and earned a high degree of someone's faith in you. Faith both to do the right thing and do the best thing, on behalf of them.

Earning the trust of a customer means that you will have both a loyal customer and a referring customer. What could be better than that? ANSWER: Two trusting customers. You get the idea.

The value of earning trust is rarely totally understood. For example, you've taken your competitor out, you got your price rather than a reduced price, you can easily get a referral, you have a loyal customer, and your reputation for being trustworthy goes through the roof.

Those five elements – no competition, no price reduction, loyalty, a referral, and an enhanced reputation – can easily double your sales and will certainly double your profit at the same time. Following this law is not an option. It's a way of life.

CAUTION: Many salespeople believe that they are trusted. Maybe even you. But my bet is that you aren't, or at least not as much as you believe you are. Go back and look at the 4.5 things you can do to build trust, and test yourself on a one to ten basis for each one. A rating of eight to ten in every category means trust is present. Anything less than an eight, you're fooling yourself.

Earn trust. You don't ask for trust. You can't force trust. You EARN trust. How are you earning it?

AHA! Trust allows loyalty to occur.

AHA! Trust is built and earned slowly over time. Not in a day. Rather, day-by-day.

AHA! The easiest way to get trust is give trust.

AHA! Trust has value way beyond money.

KEY TO IMPLEMENTATION: Start slow. Go slow. Make a list of the people who trust you. Make another list of the people who you trust. Same people? Why do you trust them? Why do they trust you? Document those elements, those reasons, those attributes, and at once you'll have a plan to build trust in others – and have them trust you.

The customer's perception of you is your reality.

JEFFREY GITOMER

15

UTILIZE VOICE OF CUSTOMERS

CHALLENGE

One customer can speak louder than a thousand salespeople. And there's a reason. People will believe other people, way more than they will believe salespeople. I mean, come on, are you going to believe the car salesman or your next-door neighbor who just bought the same car you're looking at? And it's not just true with cars, it's true in everything. Hopefully, it's true in your business. Hopefully, you're employing, and deploying, voice-of-customer videos everyplace, but especially in your sales presentations and in your social media outreach. Voice-of-customer doesn't just establish reputation, it proves it beyond any doubt. Voice-of-customer not only helps make sales, it makes them at your price. How many voices do you have selling for you?

Oh Yeah? Prove It!
Everything Requires Proof.

Can you imagine an accused criminal in a court of law, and the prosecutor says to the judge, "Your honor this man is accused of robbing a bank, but we have no proof."

The next two words the prosecutor would hear is, "Court's adjourned."

No proof, no case, no trial.

But if the defense says, "We have a witness who can corroborate the innocence of the accused," it's a different story, different outcome.

It's EXACTLY the same in sales. Not the robbing the bank part – the proof part.

If you have no proof to offer the prospective customer, you have no case, and most likely no chance to make the sale. If you have proof, you have a chance.

REALITY: When you lose a sale, it's likely you are "guilty of no proof."

So to win the sale:

- **You must employ the (video) voice of your customer to back up your claims.**

- **You must use the voice of your customer to validate your offer.**

- **You must use the voice of your customer to put a prospect's concerns to rest.**

And...

- **You must understand that your customer's voice is more powerful than yours.**

In sales, as in any court of law, you have the "burden of proof." This ensures you of credibility AND assures the customer that what you are saying is true. It goes beyond your presentation and the sale, all the way to ownership, outcome, and expected results.

Voice-of-customer – most often referred to as a *testimonial* – is THE most powerful sales tool you possess. Especially when it's in video format.

Here are the major things testimonials do, that you alone cannot do:

- **Testimonials provide a combination of proof and peace of mind.**

- **Testimonials give authentication.**

- **Testimonials offer similar, situation-proven examples.**

- **Testimonials overcome objections in a way you cannot.**

- **Testimonials offer an opportunity to get the prospective customer to change his or her perspective, and maybe change his or her mind.**

Testimonials must be specific. They must provide the "why" (others have done it) behind the "what" (you have told me).

Testimonials can provide specific information and buying motivation relating to:

- **Quality of product, company, salesperson, and service**

- **Performance after purchase – on the job outcome**

- **Productivity in your environment**

- Ease of use

- Service response time

- Value beyond price

- Longevity of product

- Loyalty of customers

- The experience of others that the customer can relate to

Which do you think is more powerful: Fight price with your words or a video testimonial about value beyond price? Overcome customer objections with your words or video testimonials that allows your customer to overcome it for you?

Testimonials have a double benefit, and a viral benefit:

1. **Testimonials are the positive proof to customers that you are who you say you are, and that your product or service will do what you claim it will do.**

2. **Testimonials build and deepen the belief of salespeople.**

2.5 **Testimonials are social media power that authenticates you in a way that the world can see.**

Here are a couple of ideas that will help you better understand what to do and how testimonials can help you make a sale:

IDEA: Make video testimonials mandatory for proposal claims. It might eliminate your competition. Especially when the testimonial is from someone that switched from them to you.

IDEA: Incorporate short video testimonials (fifteen to thirty seconds in length) into your sales presentation after every slide that makes a statement or claim.

IDEA: Your QR codes (quick response codes) should link to customer testimonials, not your boring website.

KEY POINT OF UNDERSTANDING: When making a presentation, think about what will prove your point, rather than making a weak point.

You're never alone when you make a sales call or follow up after a presentation. You can bring the voice of your customer with you. When you use the power of testimonials to eliminate lowest price, prove all your claims, eliminate competition, and build credibility, you will IMMEDIATELY avail yourself to a shorter, more profitable sales cycle.

When you say it about yourself it's bragging. When somebody else says it about you it's proof.

IF YOU BREAK THE LAW: The easiest way for you to determine if you're breaking this law or not is to study your sales presentation. Is it full of testimonials or void of testimonials?

If your answer is void, then not only have you broken the law, but you're having to send proposals, fight price, and lose to inferior competitors. The reality is a "zero-testimonial" presentation, by definition, employs old-world sales tactics and price justifications. It's a sale that you will have to fight for, rather than earn.

And if you're still looking to "find the pain," I've just given you a dose of it. Those testimonials, those voice-of-customer pieces, should appear on your website, your blog, your YouTube channel, and the rest of your social media outreach as applicable. And by the way, lack of testimonials also indicates lack of solid customer relationships, and lack of reputation.

IF YOU FOLLOW THE LAW: When you use the voice of your customers, especially in the form of testimonials, the prospect you're presenting to is better prepared to buy, they have more confidence to move forward, they don't feel they're alone, they're willing to pay your price, and they'll decide faster. Reason? You're offering undeniable proof. Third-party proof. People speaking on your behalf that are unrelated to you, other than that they buy your product or service. They're offering corroboration to your claims.

If you have enough testimonials, you wouldn't have to say word. Just hand the customer the DVD, a contract, and a pen.

CAUTION: The testimonial cannot be a pat on the head. It must address specific issues and specific values.

For example, "At first I thought their price was too high, but after I purchased, I realized that the value was amazing."

Try to make each testimonial cover a specific sales objection and end with some call to action when the customer on the video asks the customer who is watching the video to buy.

There is no more powerful voice in business and in sales than the voice of your customer.

AHA! One testimonial is worth 100 sales pitches, maybe more.

AHA! The secret of getting unlimited testimonials is easy. Earn them.

KEY TO IMPLEMENTATION: Voice-of-customer comes from customers who, for one reason or another, bought from you, paid your price, and loved the outcome so much that they're willing to talk about it.

Their testimonial comes from their gratification, their use of your product or service that went beyond their expectation, and their relationship with you.

When you're filming (on your smartphone) make sure that part of the testimonial documents specific recurring objections that other customers have had.

And be certain that each video testimonial, each voice-of-customer film clip, contains a few words about why they bought, why they love it, how they have profited from it, how much they love you, and why they're recommending it (and you) to others.

Testimonials and third-party endorsements can break a lack-of-trust barrier.

JEFFREY GITOMER

Unbreakable Law

DISCOVER THE WHY

CHALLENGE

This is the most complex of all laws because it has so many aspects, applications, and requires deep answers. Why are you doing what you do? Why are you willing to risk? Why not? Why are your earnings where they are? Why aren't they higher? Why do your customers buy? Why do your customers choose your competition? Why are people rude? Many times the answers to these questions require more than one follow-up why question. And more often than not, you don't even know why.

"I Want to Think About It."
"I Want to Think It Over." Crap!

You go through your ENTIRE, one-hour, amazing sales presentation. You nailed it. The prospect seemed to be in agreement, even excited at times.

He or she had all the logical and emotional reasons to buy, but at the end of your pitch said, "Sounds great. I need to think it over for a few days."

RATS!

Now what? Say something? Use a worn out sales technique? Agree and leave? Offer to call back or come back in a few days?

Meanwhile you're pissed off, off balance, and about to make a bad choice. Add to that you're mentally blaming the customer for his indecisiveness. Relax.

I'm about to share 2.5 definitive answers to this age-old sales barrier:

1. **Why it occurs.**
2. **What to do about it.**
2.5 **What never to do about it.**

Why do prospects say, "I want to think about it"? Most salespeople never understand or are never taught why the *think it over* situation occurs.

It is a direct result of one or more of these reasons:

- **There's an unspoken fear or reason.**
- **There's a perceived risk.**
- **They don't want to "just say no."**
- **They're not the real decision maker.**
- **You haven't uncovered the real motive to buy.**
- **They don't like you.**

- **They don't believe you.**
- **They don't have confidence in you.**
- **They don't trust you.**
- **They think your price is too high.**
- **They can't afford what you're selling.**

These reasons why are the real barrier. "I want to think about it" is a stall or a mask, not an objection or a barrier.

GOOD NEWS: Many of these elements are discoverable WAY before you get to the end of your presentation.

But it's up to you to understand what really causes "think it over." It's YOU!

In over thirty years of sales training, I've never heard ONE salesperson say, "The guy said I want to think about it, and it was all my fault!"

It's not about RESPONSE.
It's about PREVENTION.

Before you blame the customer for their inability to decide, ask yourself:

- **Did I offer a value proposition that favored the customer?**
- **Did I ask enough questions to discover their motive and urgency to buy?**
- **Did I establish rapport and friendly dialogue?**
- **Was I able to create a perceived difference between me and my competition?**
- **Did I uncover the prospect's experience and past use?**
- **Do I know the prospect's expected outcome?**

Before you hear the words "I want to think about it" from a prospective customer, you may be able to prevent it. Study the reasons above as a start. They are the major clues as to the root cause.

TAKE NOTE: With the Internet, social media, and your responsibility to build a visible reputation, combined with your ability to find everything you need to prepare for your sales call, you must be prepared in terms of the customer. And your reputation must precede you.

Reputation and preparation in terms of the customer – and how they win from the acquisition of your product or service – will reduce and eliminate doubt. These are major causes of "think it over."

RULE: Never use an old-world technique to force or rush the sale. You'll not only lose the sale, you'll also lose respect. Rather, try to uncover the emotional or real cause of indecision.

REALITY: Do they want to think about price or just get rid of you?

REALITY: "I want to think it over" is often a red flag for "your price is too high" or "I want to try to get a better deal."

REALITY: Rather than try a sales tactic, try to ascertain an understanding of why, so you can prevent the objection next time.

RESILIENCE: If the prospect says "I want to think it over" ask them how long they feel they need, and make a firm, written down appointment to return in person.

If you're able to create a perceived difference in the mind of the buyer between your product or service and the others, and if you are able to create a perceived value in the mind of the buyer between your product or service and the others – then you have a chance.

If the prospect likes you, believes you, has confidence in you, and trusts you – there's likely to be a sale.

Think that over.

Decisions, Decisions.
How Good at Them Are You?

Decisions – either by you, your coworker, your boss, your family members, or your customer – drive your success, your lifestyle, and your attitude.

As you're contemplating what to do, or how to decide, there are stream-of-consciousness thoughts that affect the final choice and the resulting outcome.

Whether you're buying something, working on a project, parenting, or making a sale, there are decisions you have to make that will determine the outcome. Your job is to make the best one. The right one.

Most people think decisions are made based on economics. The price. But most people are wrong. Decisions are made based on a myriad of elements and price is only one of them. Perceived value is much more of a factor than price.

The majority of decisions you make are based on existing emotion and perception combined with previous experience – UNLESS you're in politics or corporate politics.

Those (political) decisions are made based on what's popular, what's likely to be approved, what's safe (nobody ever got fired for buying IBM), or what's politically expedient – and almost NEVER based on what's best for the whole country or company.

If you're willing to think deeper about the decision-making process for yourself, it may help you understand how others make their decisions. In a career like yours where your income is based on the decisions of others, this is key.

Regardless of the decision at hand – yes, no, put off, act, buy, don't buy, date, or reject – the questions on the next page will help your conscious and subconscious mind understand your decision-making process AND help you understand the decision-making process of others.

Here are some of the thoughts that enter your mind as you make choices:

- **What's the circumstance?**
- **What's the reason?**
- **What's the motive?**
- **What's the risk?**
- **What are my fears?**
- **What's the reward?**
- **What's the real issue?**
- **What's the real barrier?**
- **What's the money?**
- **What's the perceived value?**
- **What's the measurable value?**
- **What's the social value?**
- **What's the objective?**
- **What is my desired result?**
- **What am I hoping for?**
- **What is the outcome likely to be?**
- **What if it isn't?**
- **Who gets hurt?**
- **Who benefits?**
- **What are the elements?**
- **What has been my past experience?**
- **What is my experience-based knowledge?**
- **Should I counsel anyone?**
- **Do I have to decide now?**
- **Is this temporary or permanent?**
- **Do I trust the other person?**
- **What's the deadline or the urgency?**
- **What is my gut telling me?**

Keep in mind all decisions involve some sort of risk. Risk involves and creates fear. The greater the risk, the more measured, deliberate, and collaborative the process. It's always a judgment call, and fear often interferes with sound judgment.

IMPORTANT NOTE: The decision to buy is made emotionally, and then justified logically. You make the decision and then defend it – sometimes to a fault.

The words "no brainer" have always bothered me in the decision-making process. When someone says, "It's a no brainer" to me I become alarmed. What they're saying is, "Don't think about it, just do it." Not good. All decisions are "brainers."

On the positive side of "decide," when you make a decision, ask yourself:

- **Am I doing what's best for myself (or for my company)?**
- **Am I taking the high road?**
- **Am I choosing the best value?**
- **Am I at peace with myself?**

On the negative side of "decide," ask yourself:

- **Am I making an excuse to do it, even though I doubt the validity of it?**
- **Am I justifying it before the facts are gathered?**
- **Am I justifying it after the fact, and I knew it was a mistake?**
- **Am I procrastinating?**
- **Am I saying, "It's the lesser of two evils"?**
- **Am I only getting buy-in before the fact to mitigate blame?**

NOTE WELL: Fear of loss is greater than desire to gain. Fear of being wrong is more powerful than risk of being right.

As you're trying to get others to decide on you and your product or service, keep top of mind how *you* make decisions.

The better you understand yourself, the more powerful you'll be at "getting a favorable decision" from others.

JEFFREY GITOMER

How to Discover the Real Why?

As a child, you rarely found out the real why, even though you asked.

Your mom or your dad gave you an order or command of some kind, and you immediately whined, "Why?" Unfortunately, their answer was often "because I said so" or "because I'm your mother."

That was the lesson that taught you discovery of the real why is much more difficult to attain than just by asking.

Fast forward twenty years, and now your business cards are printed. The word "why" becomes even more important in every aspect of the success of your sales career.

When you ask a question of the customer to determine if they're going to buy or not, no matter whether they say yes or no, you must still understand "why" they are moving forward, or "why not."

The purpose of uncovering and understanding why is two-fold:

1. **To find out exactly where you are with the customer and why you're there.**

2. **So that on the next sales call, your increased why understanding will result in better communication, better rapport, and ultimately a better outcome.**

BEWARE AND BE AWARE: Finding out why or why not takes courage and a real relationship.

If you're reluctant to find out why a customer did or did not buy, the prime reason is that your relationship is weak and you're afraid to lose it by getting a bit more personal and a bit deeper in the engagement process.

Nothing could be further from the truth.

Your prime responsibility as a salesperson is to gain greater understanding of all your customers so you may build a wealth of knowledge.

Here's a strategy you can employ to avoid using the actual word "why," and still uncover why. Ask the customer a question that begins with: *what made you choose,* or *how do you determine,* or *what has your experience been,* or *was there one incident that you could point to that clarified your thinking?*

This type of question asks the customer for their wisdom, their knowledge, and their experience.

Their response will not only answer your why question, it will also give you additional insight as to their thinking and the way they perceive you, your product, your company, and your relationship.

The word "why" is almost accusatory, therefore it's better to couch your phrases and your questions so that you find out why without ever using the word.

You must know the customer's why, and you must use every tactical skill you possess, especially your questions, in order to uncover it.

IF YOU BREAK THE LAW: If you don't discover the why, you'll be trying to sell when all the customer wants to do is buy, and you may never meet. Why is the dominant driver to the purchase. AND... if you don't know your own why, your belief system will not be powerful enough to make real sales. Doubt causes hesitation – both in offering and asking, and in the self-confidence to make things happen. Discovering why requires thought and self-truth to start, and superior questioning and reasoning skills thereafter. Breaking this law has a high cost to yourself, a high cost of lost sales, and an element of "blame" that goes with both.

IF YOU FOLLOW THE LAW: Getting to why both for yourself and your customers provides a huge learning breakthrough. The key word here is *understanding*. It's also a career breakthrough that will garner a huge amount of sales and genuine relationships. When the customer feels and perceives that you understand them, their emotion kicks in, and orders will begin to fly across the desk and the Internet – landing in your lap!

CAUTION: Your why is constant. Your customer's why (their motive to buy) can have a thousand variations. Each customer's why must be discovered separately and acted on with emotional empathy.

AHA! Understanding your own why, your own motives, will help you uncover the why of others.

AHA! Without understanding a customer's motive to buy, their why, you'll be selling price forever.

AHA! Knowing why customers buy is one billion times more powerful than knowing how to sell.

What you're trying to sell is meaningless, unless you understand why the customer wants to buy it.

MAJOR AHA! When you understand why, you immediately uncover motive and speed up the sales cycle simultaneously. When the prospect's why is uncovered and understood, buyer urgency is apparent.

KEY TO IMPLEMENTATION: Before you can ever uncover and understand your customer's why motive, you better uncover and understand your own. Uncovering your own why will not just teach you the process, it will also show you the emotion attached to the discovery. Understanding how to get the emotional "why" will set you apart from 95% of others, and give you sales power you won't believe.

Finding out the "why" behind the "what" of your presentation is one of the most important aspects in building relationships, understanding customers, and making more sales.

JEFFREY GITOMER

INTEND TO ACHIEVE

CHALLENGE

Tons and tons, and even more tons, have been written about setting and achieving goals. Almost nothing has been written about intentions. Intentions are the foundation for goal achievement. Intentions are the power behind goal achievement. Intentions create both resolve and desire. The resolve and desire to achieve. What are your intentions? When you get your sales plan or sales quota, do you intend to achieve it? Or are you defeated the moment you look at it?

Success vs. Fulfillment.
Which Is It for You?

People make goals, life choices, career choices, and business choices – even relationship choices – based in large part on their tolerance for risk weighted against their greed. As life progresses, these decisions will be mitigated and compromised based on existing conditions of family and debt. Often not in that order.

When you're young you have goals and dreams, often verbalized by the statement, "When I grow up, I want to be a (fill in the blank)." As you mature, you may change your mind, based on your life experiences.

Here are the elements of achievement:

- **You have a drive.**

- **You have a desire.**

- **You have a goal.**

- **You have a dream.**

- **Your dream may be different than your goal.**

Your *goal* may be to make your quota, or become the number-one salesperson in your company. But your *dream* may be to live by the ocean or start your own business.

THE QUESTION IS: Do you have a love for what you are striving for, and is it the same love as what you're dreaming for?

Love drives true passion.
Passion drives achievement.

If you don't love what you do, odds are you will not achieve your goal, let alone your dream. Why would you put that much energy into something you don't love? The answer is: you probably wouldn't. Love is also the breeding ground for *intention*. And intention is the first step in achievement.

Why do you want to succeed? What are your success intentions?
- **For the money?**
- **For the safety?**
- **For the status?**
- **To show others?**
- **For short-term gratification?**
- **For the greed of having success at the expense of happiness?**

Or are your intentions more honorable and more personally gratifying?
- **Are you striving to be the best at what you do?**
- **Do you have real passion for what you do?**

You often hear people described as "driven." I would rather hear "he has passion" or "she loves what he does."

Over the years, I have given audiences an opportunity to comment on my sales seminars. I ask them what they liked best, I ask them what they intend to do tomorrow, and I ask them for a candid comment.

As you can imagine, I have received comments all across the board from hundreds of thousands of people, but the ones I cherish most all say the same thing, "Jeffrey loves what he does and it shows." That's a compliment that has no peers.

What do you love? Not *who* do you love.

For many, who you love changes over time.

For those of you (me included) who have children, they are who you love – forever and unconditionally. And hopefully, you love yourself.

What you love is different. What you love leads to success AND fulfillment.

You know what it is you love at the moment. Think about what you do with passion. Play ball, ski, travel, sew, read, golf, race. Don't you love it? Then think about what sports team you love to watch, or who you cheer for. How much do you (or would you) pay to see them play?

The real "what do you love" questions are:

- **Do you love what you do for a living?**

- **Do you love your career?**

- **Do you love your job?**

Passion needs to be discovered – then unleashed. "What do you love?" is easily discovered. You've heard the expressions: "He found his passion," "He found his true calling," and "She's a natural."

When you love what you do, it's not just self-evident, it's evident to others. Your enthusiasm is transferable. One of the best saleswomen I ever met talked to me about her love of sales and love of job. She said, "I do everything full force." Me? I say it a slightly different way, "I strive to do my best at what I love to do." How do you say it? How do you feel about it?

MAJOR CLUE: Every day your road to fulfillment starts in the bathroom. And every day, whether you realize it or not, you can take the "Bathroom Mirror Test." All you have to do is ask and answer these 4.5 critical questions – every day:

1. **Am I happy on the inside?**

2. **Am I doing what I love?**

3. **Am I doing my best for those I love?**

4. **Am I doing my best for myself?**

4.5. **Am I smiling?**

This is not a sales lesson. It's a life lesson. Sales is just part of life. If you love what you do, your passion will lead you to success, and your success will lead to your fulfillment.

KEY INSIGHT THAT WILL DRIVE YOUR ACTIONS: Beyond your goals, to-do list, and urgent matters of the day, it's your INTENTIONS that drive your actions – both daily and long term. Intentions precede actions and are the mental drivers to achievement. In short: you only do what you intend to do. As you think about your priorities and prepare your list of "must dos," identify and affirm your willingness and your intention to make the priorities happen, or you will find a convenient excuse for failure.

IF YOU BREAK THE LAW: If you don't intend, you won't achieve. The main reason goals are not achieved is simple: you didn't intend to achieve them. Breaking the law of intentions has major consequences. Not the least of which is that it tends to spill over into all other aspects of your life, and you become complacent. *If I do it that's okay, and if I don't do it that's okay too.* Not good. Actually, dangerous.

Lack of intention is a self-fulfilling prophecy. It's not what you have to do, it's what you intend to do. Once you understand intention, once you understand the power of intention, you can see new possibilities at once. Not just possibilities for achieving a specific goal, but a true understanding for what it takes to achieve any goal.

IF YOU FOLLOW THE LAW: I believe you now see the importance of intention, and what role it plays in your achievement and your life. Once you decide to be more deliberate in what you intend to do, the plans become easier, the actions come easier, and the success becomes self-evident. Once you intend, you achieve.

CAUTION: Intention is a very subtle thought, and may be a new one for you. To understand it better, look at it as determination, or drive, or focus, or even just making a plan for success. But unless you actually define intention both in your mind and on paper, it may not become a habit. The habit of intention creates the atmosphere for achievement. Your achievement.

AHA! When I first realized the power of intention, I immediately applied it to two specific projects that for one reason or another had fallen to procrastination. Both are now complete. One was an ebook, and one was a customer follow-up. Both are now money. Think of intention as money.

AHA! Mentally change "gonna" to "intend." I'm gonna lose ten pounds. I intend to lose ten pounds. Which do you think is more powerful? Intention makes things happen.

KEY TO IMPLEMENTATION: Here's a way to begin understanding intention: Take a resolution or a goal that you did not achieve. Write down why that achievement did not occur. Not excuses, the real why. Now write another paragraph on what you could have intended to do that might've made that goal, or that resolution, a reality.

You may have a goal, or you may have been given a goal, but your intentions will dictate the outcome of the effort (or lack of it).

JEFFREY GITOMER

BE PERCEIVED
AS DIFFERENT

CHALLENGE

If the customer doesn't perceive a difference, there is NONE, regardless of your rhetoric. It may be in your speed of response, it may be in a service offering you have, it may be same-day shipping, OR NOT. It may be as simple as answering your phone with a live person. Wanna know what your real difference is? Go get your customer's perception of why you're different. Their perception is the only one that matters.

If You're Different, They Will Buy. How Different Are You?

"Tell me why I should buy from you."

When the vice president of a prominent New York City based perfume manufacturer put that challenge to me (earlier in my career), it was about why he should buy my T-shirt for his huge promotion rather than one of the sample garments he had piled up desk-high from my competitors.

I smiled, opened my briefcase, and threw him a piece of fabric in the exact shade of their corporate color.

I said, "That pile of shirts behind you is all samples of what THEY make. My worthy competition is selling you their shirt with your imprint. We make the garment YOU want. We start with the finest interlock fabric, dye it to your color, cut and sew it to your measurements, and imprint it to your exact specifications."

"How do you know what size a 'medium' is? How wide is the body?" I said as I casually showed him a few of my fully sewn garments in each size so he could see the difference in body width and style of construction – different stitching, different neck cuts, different sleeve cuts. I continued as he began to lean forward and pay attention.

"What's the price?" he semi-demanded.

"Forty-two fifty a dozen." I zapped back.

"Forty-two fifty a dozen?!" He screamed. "Your competition is $36.00 or less."

"Oh, You want those crappy shirts – we can sell you those for $32.50 a dozen," I quipped with a smile. "But if you're looking for something your customers will wear with the same pride as they wear your perfume, I recommend you invest in the quality of the product, not the price."

Silence.

"How personalized can you make it?" he challenged.

"Order 5,000 dozen and we'll put in your own label," I said without hesitating a split second.

"What would you do for 8,000 dozen?" He dangled the carrot.

"Put them in individual polybags at no additional cost." I dangled back with a big smile.

"When do you want delivery?" I closed.

"Twelve weeks." He smiled.

"When can I get a purchase order?" I said in the firmest voice I could muster.

"How about now?" He said straight-faced.

"Now would be fine," I said, with every bit of my innards jumping for joy but outside still giving the cool-as-a-cucumber look.

And I sat there as he wrote me the PO and shoved it across the desk. Victory, baby. Victory. (Yes, I admit I did the calculator thing: $42.50 times 8,000 times my commission.)

THE LESSON: How did I make that sale?

I made the sale because I was different, creative, willing to take a risk or two, and perceived to be more valuable than my competition.

"Why should I buy from you?" Every prospect asks that question either verbally or silently. If there's one question you must be perpetually ready to answer, it's that one.

Here are the 7.5 elements that made my sale possible, and I challenge you to see how many of those elements you are using when your prospect "pops the question."

1. I knew I was up against others with the same product, so I went in with a different approach and what I felt was a winning idea. That one won. They all don't win. But you have to walk in with ideas.

2. I had all the answers to his objections pre-prepared. I knew what all the objections were. So do you. Have them answered in advance or lose to someone who does.

3. I had a surprise (the piece of cloth rather than the shirt). People like surprises.

4. I had a higher price and a reason to buy it. My reason was not just greater quality, it was also greater personalization.

5. I was sure of my answers at every turn. I knew my product and I knew my deal-making parameters before I walked in the door.

6. I created the visualization of a successful outcome. People buy with an outcome in mind. Your job is not only to know your product and your capabilities. Your job is also to get the prospect to see the successful result of purchase.

7. I knew the buying signals when they were offered. After he dropped the price objection, he asked the questions with the "intent to buy," not the "intention to know." Big difference.

7.5 I assumed I had the sale from the start, and asked for it when it was time to ask. "When is the right time?" you ask. Boy, I wish I knew the stock answer for that one. That's why this is the .5 part of the list. You need to trust your instinct. The secret is in the preparation. The more prepared you are when you enter the door, the more you will "feel" when the time is right, Luke.

May the sale be with you.

Differentiate with value, or die with price.

JEFFREY GITOMER

We're Different. I Swear, We're Different.

Go get a pen and paper.

Make a list of EVERYTHING that you claim about your company and your product or service that your competition does NOT claim they do or have. Go ahead, make a list. Nothing yet?

Then name ONE THING that you claim to have, that your competition won't claim they have. Great quality? They claim that. Great service? They claim that too. Great delivery? They claim that too. Great people? They claim that too. You say tomato, I say tomahto – but the prospect perceives the same thing.

Here are a few painful questions:

- **What's different about what you offer?**
- **What's different about what your literature says?**
- **What's different in your creative approach or ideas?**
- **What's different in the ordinary things you do?**

If the customer does not perceive a difference, you think the answer is (all that's left is) "price." And price is ALWAYS the wrong answer.

If you sell lowest price, there is no loyalty. It's a transaction, not a sale.

And the next salesperson who stumbles in one penny lower takes your commission away. Lowest price also means lowest profit.

MAJOR CLUE: If you're having difficulty in making business relationships, it means you aren't distinguishable enough to earn a chance.

"Rats, Jeffrey," you say, "How do I get different?" There are answers, and they require some hard work. BUT, if you're willing to work at it, I can guarantee long-term victory.

Here are the answers:

- **The difference is the prospect's perception of YOU as a person.** The salesperson is the first sale made. If they don't buy the difference in you, you have no chance for the rest.

- **The difference is the prospect's perceived "higher value" in dealing with you.** The higher the perceived value, the less price matters. If the prospect perceives the product as relatively the same, then value creation both in the front of the sale and after the sale are the only true differentiators.

- **The difference is creativity.** At the core of differentiation is the science of creativity and your free time to brainstorm the possibilities, either alone or in a group of peers.

Everyone says to be creative you gotta "think outside the box." And everyone is wrong. To master creativity, I recommend you start by thinking INSIDE the box first.

Inside the box? What's that supposed to mean? Easy – to learn the science of being different start with the obvious. If your everyday communications are just like your competitor's, why should they believe you when you say "we're different"?

There are many opportunities to be perceived as different. Here are three BIG ones – that have to do with your ability to be perceived as different through your daily actions, communications, and ability to create value:

1. **The creative sales approach you take.** How you present your product or service – that's the difference the prospect perceives between you and the others he has seen.

2. **The ordinary (daily) expressions of business.** How you greet, message, web, and brochure yourselves.

3. **Customer communications and actions in service areas.** When something goes wrong, differentiation is the key element. You may know it as the WOW! factor, but with all the lousy service these days, just something "above mediocre" will get attention. And if you don't think that great service can make a difference in the growth and profitability of a company, call Dillard's and ask them about Nordstrom. Call BMW and ask them about Lexus.

Okay, okay, so, Jeffrey, how do we differentiate?

There are 14.5 "inside the box" elements you should think about and take action on today.

THE TEST HERE IS: Will what you do be talked about after the impression passes? Will anyone say, "Hey look at this, you gotta see this!" or, "You gotta hear this!" If no one is saying anything, it's a dud – and so are you.

Be different in the comfort of your office:

1. Your voicemail message is dull. Sharpen it. Are you either on your phone or away from your desk? Are you telling people what day of the week it is? Is the message on your voicemail great or average? Get great.

2. Your office greeting and phone transfer. Are your people friendly? Is a computer answering your phone and making your customer mad before he gets to you? Does it transfer people to voicemail hell? Offer options before you transfer a call.

3. After hours messaging. Is it fun? Does it page someone? Do you direct me to your website for action? Or does it just say, "We're closed, duh."

4. Ease of ordering or doing business with you. Call your office and try to place an order. Try to get a salesperson. Try to get yourself. After hours ordering? (ouch)

5. Eat, drink, and be merry. Your office coffee. Your snacks and in-house food. Serve the best, not the cheapest.

To be different in your corporate communication:

6. The save-ability of your literature. Is your info all about you or is it information the prospect will keep because it's valuable? Useful information gets passed around. Does all info about you find its way to the trash?

7. Change your business card. Now. Fast. "I can't," you whine. "The company provides them this way." Just print "SEE OTHER SIDE" on your card or change your title to something fun or compelling. Is your prospect showing it to someone else because it's so cool? Get cool.

8. Are your ads bragging or proof? Advertising is great if you use testimonials to tell your story. Most people just brag about themselves. Pity.

9. The front page of your website. Is the information on it about the customer or all about you? We-we websites get one visit. Creative websites attract word-of-mouth advertising and return visits (or the ultimate victory: "bookmarked").

To catch fire in the heat of the sale:

10. Revise the opening line of your cold calls. If you're forced to make them, ask for the sales department instead of your normal "I'd like to speak to the person in charge of..." drivel. Salespeople will tell you everything, direct you to the right person, and help you open the door.

11. Change the opening of your sales presentation. Start with a series of questions and ideas. Don't give your name or card until you have stimulated so much interest that the prospect says, "Who are you?"

12. Reverse the messages you leave for others. Ask questions about their issues, give two great facts and get them to call you for the third. Is the current message you leave for others all about them or about the money you want from them?

13. Follow up after a sales call or a proposal submission with value, not insincerity. "I'm calling to see if you have any questions." Whenever someone says that to me I ask them who won the world series in 1984. They rarely know, but always laugh (Baltimore Orioles). Stop calling people to find out how your money is doing. Offer information that is valuable. Show them you have ideas and enthusiasm for THEIR stuff, not just yours.

14. How are you staying in front of a customer after (between) sales? How about an emailed tip of the week? Something that helps THEM.

14.5 Tell me (show me) you love me. Customers want an initial feeling of warmth. What feeling do you give? How are calls answered at your place? If a computer answers your phone, everything I have said is worthless until you rip that device out of the wall. Everyone HATES it when a computer answers the phone. The trend is to return to the human "hello." Your friendliness (or lack of it) will determine your future.

REALITY: Salespeople want to differentiate, prove value, be memorable, make the sale, stay in touch, build the relationship, and earn a referral. That's what Ace of Sales does. It's a game-changer, and a sales-maker. Go to www.aceofsales.com, try it for thirty days on me, and start real differentiation today.

IF YOU BREAK THE LAW: If you find yourself constantly in a price battle, it ain't the price, it's you and your inability to differentiate yourself from the competition you're fighting against. Fundamentally, this sounds pretty obvious, but realistically this tragic flaw happens everyday to everyone in sales, including you. If you know you have to be different, and you know you have to prove it to the customer, then the answer is obvious: build proof into your presentation. It's not rocket science, it's way more powerful than rocket science. It's sales science, and your job is to execute it.

IF YOU FOLLOW THE LAW: When you can prove differentiation to a prospective customer, they gain confidence in you, they believe you, and they begin to have a vision of doing business with you. They're thinking, "clearly this guy's product is different than/better than the others I've seen." And the best part is, you don't have to ask customers what they perceive as the difference. They will begin to ask you questions about delivery and ownership. Also known as buying signals.

If the customer perceives no difference between you and the competition, all that's left is price.

AHA! As you are contemplating what to prove, think about your biggest customer needs and your biggest customer demands. Prove those.

AHA! Perceived difference is one of two major stepping-stones toward making the sale at your price. The other is perceived value.

AHA! Don't tell me you're different – prove it!

KEY TO IMPLEMENTATION: Knowing your "difference" does not come from you, it comes from the PERCEPTION of your customers. If you REALLY wanna know where your difference lies, go ask 'em. Ask a few dozen customers, record their answers on a video on your smart phone. Now you have "difference" nailed from the mind of one customer to another. That's a difference you can take to the bank.

At the core of differentiation is the science of creativity and your free time to brainstorm the possibilities – either alone or in a group of peers.

JEFFREY GITOMER

Unbreakable Law

19

PERFORM DYNAMICALLY

CHALLENGE

The weakest area of most salespeople is their presentation skills. If you possess all the knowledge on the planet, but you have poor presentation skills, your message fall on deaf ears. Think back to college and your most brilliant professor. How impactful were his or her presentation skills in class lectures? They were often the difference between paying attention and not paying attention. It's no different with your customers. To me, having excellent presentation skills is a given. But the sad reality is that presentation skills are rarely taught or emphasized.

MAJOR CLUE: Once you become proficient at presenting, the real potential for your increased sales power lies in your ability to convert your presentation into a dynamic performance.

How Have You Progressed Since Third Grade?

"What I did on my summer vacation."

Every one of you has given a speech or written a paragraph or essay about what you did on your summer vacation while you were in grade school.

You wrote about the lake, the mountains, or the week at the beach. Or you gave a speech and your opening line was, "What I did on my summer vacation." And you held your own hands and nervously performed in front of your peers.

You were worried about what they would think and you were nervous about performing in front of your classmates, but somehow you muddled through it.

Your essay was returned with all kinds of red marks for punctuation, grammar, and misspellings.

For those of you who are pack rats, or have parents who are pack rats, you may still have the document.

PERSONAL NOTE: I have many of my daughters' early writings. All gems.

I'm giving you this reminder, this bit of nostalgic instant memory, so I can issue you the following challenges: How have you progressed since then? How much better are your writing skills? How much better are your presentation skills? And how important are those skills to your sales success, your business success, your social media success, and your career success?

I've been a professional writer and speaker for over twenty-five years. But like you, I was an amateur in the third grade when I talked about what I did on my summer vacation, and I was in the fourth grade when I wrote about Hurricane Hazel which rocked Atlantic City where my family was living at the time. (If you Google it, you can figure out how old I am!)

What most people don't understand is their initial training forms the foundation of their present skills. Your grammar, your ability to spell, your self-confidence to be able to speak to others, as well as both small and large groups, and your overall character are formulated by your ability to communicate both orally and in writing.

Every one of you reading this is now thinking, *maybe I should have paid more attention* when my high school English teacher was drilling the difference of there, their, and they're or the difference of your and you're.

Think about the emails you receive with the subject line that says: "Your in Luck!"

The person who wrote it is immediately perceived as an idiot and the email is discarded as both disingenuous and poorly prepared.

Maybe I'm prejudiced, but I am hesitant to do business with someone who can't correct his or her own work in the simplest subject line of an email.

The reason I'm harping on speaking and writing is because they are the foundation of the two most important elements of your success: image and reputation. Everyone wants to have a great image. Everyone wants to have a great reputation.

GOOD NEWS IS: You can influence both your image and your reputation with your CONSISTENT performance.

When I ask my audiences, "How many of you would be nervous speaking in front of a group of 300 people?" almost everyone raises his or her hand. But the real issue isn't that they're nervous or uncomfortable. Those are symptoms. The real issue is they are UNPREPARED. They lack the experience, the subject matter expertise, or suffer from limited self-image or low self-esteem – or perhaps all four.

This is further complicated by the fact that most of you reading this know what show is on television on Wednesday night at nine o'clock, and you're glued to the set to witness the next episode of "other people's drama." You make a conscious choice to watch something rather than to learn something or do something.

Perhaps if you took a Dale Carnegie course on public speaking or joined a Toastmasters group, you would be able to become a confident presenter.

Perhaps if you started your own blog, and at the age of thirty or forty you write about what you did on your summer vacation, you might be able to attract people with similar likes and values as they search the Internet the same way you do.

Please do not confuse this with a call to action. Rather, it's a call to reality.

REALITY: Your writing skills and your speaking skills need to be at a higher level of competence if you are looking to elevate your income.

REALITY: Your reputation is the sum total of your words and deeds – a large portion of which can come from writing and speaking.

Your customer is more likely to buy your message if they buy into your passion.

REALITY: You can gain an amazing business social media presence if you combine your ability to write and your ability to convey a value message to your customers.

Here's my 2.5-part recommendation to you...

1. Write a 500-word blog post once a week. Write about something you love. Write about something that may impact your customers. Write about something you have expertise in.

2. Speak in public once a week. A civic organization will be happy to have you as their breakfast or lunch presenter. Speak on something you love, speak on something others will value, or speak on something in which you are an expert.

2.5 You will not reap immediate rewards. But slowly over time your dynamic performance ability will emerge. That's a reward that has nothing to do with commissions or earnings, but it has everything to do with the feeling of fulfillment. That's a feeling I hope you get to experience.

Salespeople make the fatal mistake of making a presentation. It's not a presentation; it's a performance.

JEFFREY GITOMER

How Lousy Are You?
You Probably Don't Even Know!

I have spent the last sixty or so odd years watching local television commercials, and the last thirty years listening to thousands of sales pitches and speeches at meetings and training sessions.

The one thing a good portion of presenters and speakers have in common is *lousy presentation skills.*

BIG QUESTION: How important are presentation skills? Maybe a better question is: How important are YOUR presentation skills?

BIGGER QUESTIONS: How excellent are your presentation skills on a scale of 1 to 100? Do people WANT to listen to you? Or do they HAVE to listen to you?

BIGGEST QUESTIONS: How are you improving your speaking and presentation skills? What are you doing to increase your ability to persuade and convince? How transferable is your message? Are people moved to take action after you present?

These questions not only beg answers; your answers also provide a report card of your present situation.

Funny, if you got a bad report card in grade school, high school, or college, your parents would have made you study harder, take remedial classes, and do more homework. Now that you're out of school, and your business cards are printed, you have ignored the success strategy that made you a better and more successful student.

Now is the time that superior presentation skills really count.

If you improve your speaking skills at work, you can easily measure the outcome and results – in money.

Here's a short list of why presenters and presentations fail:

- **Lousy choice of words**
- **Lousy vocal variety**
- **Lousy gesturing**
- **Lousy body language**
- **Lousy smiles**
- **Lousy sincerity**
- **Lousy choice of structure**
- **Lousy passion stemming from a poor belief system.**

There are many other sale-killing elements in a presentation. At the top of the list are lousy, boring, crowded, PowerPoint slides.

There are a few other points of understanding that create a negative atmosphere during a talk or presentation:

- **Condescending hand gestures**
- **Inability to relax**
- **Having to read or memorize from your head, rather than giving your presentation from your heart**

Okay, that's the bad news. Here's the remedy!

The key points of a great presentation are:

- **Knowing what you want to say**
- **Believing what you say**
- **Being believable and convincing**
- **Being compelling in how you say it**
- **Providing valuable information**
- **Providing useable information**
- **Providing timely information**
- **Being completely prepared and rehearsed**

If you're not that good, let others speak for you.

Why does every car commercial have a bad announcer (or an equally bad owner) giving the hype about how low the price is, how great the deal is, or how much you'll save? Why not let five customers talk for ten seconds each?

HERE'S THE STRATEGY FOR DYNAMIC PERFORMANCES: Make your message transferable. The audience, whether it's one or one thousand, must say to themselves, "I get it. I agree with it. I think I can do it. I'm willing to try it." Or "I get it. I like it. I understand why I need or want it. My risk tolerance is low. I'm willing to buy it."

HERE'S THE SECRET: Record yourself. If you make a video recording of your presentation and watch it twice, you will see for yourself just how good or bad you are. I have found this to be the only way to determine strengths and flaws. It will also give you an opportunity to make an improvement game plan.

Poor presentation skills costing you sales, loyalty, morale, and reputation? If you're looking to get back in the game, great speaking and presentation skills can be your weapons of mass introduction.

GREAT NEWS: Most corporate presenters and sales presenters are deplorable. This gives you an amazing opportunity to capture your market by captivating your audience.

Dynamic Speaking and Presentations Are Not an Option.

I give more than seventy-five presentations a year at annual meetings and sales meetings. There are always other presenters. CEOs and VPs of everything from finance to marketing.

Most of the speakers are (to be kind) less than compelling. Most of the speakers (to be unkind) are boring. People in the audience are doing emails and texting while their CEO is speaking. YIKES.

These companies have paid hundreds of thousands of dollars to put on these meetings, and their messages may not be getting through.

My philosophy of speaking and speakers has always been – the person in the front of the room giving a speech has a responsibility to be DYNAMIC. He or she must have a compelling, transferable message that creates action on the part of each audience member.

They may be a brilliant leader, they may be a brilliant marketer or CFO, but the audience is elsewhere during their talk.

REALITY: If you're a leader in front of your people, ask yourself this: Do they WANT to listen to me, or do they HAVE to listen to me?

The answer to that question is the harsh reality of your speaking and presentation skills.

Here are the primary reasons speakers fall flat:

- **Lack of training in public speaking**
- **Lack of preparedness**
- **Lack of material mastery**
- **Lack of rehearsal**
- **Lack of understanding of speech responsibility**
- **Lack of understanding the audience**
- **Boring material**
- **No humor**
- **Excuse-based speech (nervous, not enough time to prepare, bad slides, bad room, bad time of day)**

Tons of books have been written on the subject of speaking and presentations. Dale Carnegie wrote one of the most famous, called simply, *Public Speaking*. It was written in 1926, and it's still in print eighty-seven years later.

One of the most informative and one of the earliest pieces written about public speaking was by the father of self-help in America, Orison Swett Marden.

Marden's classic book is Pushing to the Front, *published in 1911. In chapter 33, entitled "Self-Improvement through Public Speaking," he espouses wisdom like:*

- **"No matter how much you may know about a subject, if it does not happen to interest those to whom you are talking, your efforts will be largely lost."**
- **"No amount of natural ability or education or good clothes, no amount of money, will make you appear well if you cannot express yourself in good language."**
- **"One's judgment, education, manhood, character, all the things that go to make a man what he is, are being unrolled like a panorama in his efforts to express himself."**

- **"In thinking on one's feet before an audience, one must think quickly, vigorously, effectively. This requires practice and experience early in life."**

- **"Every time you rise to your feet you will increase your confidence, and after a while you will form the habit of speaking until it will be as easy as anything else."**

Sound advice that's available for free. The entire book is now in the public domain. (It may be the best personal development book of all time.)

I ask executives how much public speaking training they have had, and the usual response is, "Little or none." WHY?

Many look at public speaking and presentations as "unimportant," or try to let their PowerPoint slides speak for them. BAD decision.

Before you go off on me, let me say this: "There are many dynamic executive presenters!" Just not that many.

I have some ideas that will help you:

- **Take a course.** You can jump-start your ability by educating yourself.

- **Speak in safe venues.** Civic groups. Or in front of your coworkers.

- **Hire a coach.** Someone who has been there often, and done it dynamically.

- **Film yourself EVERY TIME YOU SPEAK.** Filming is the ONLY path to self-improvement.

- **Master your slides if you use them.** Slides can make or break a talk.

- **Master your speech.** Live rehearsal, and total belief in what you're saying is integral to authenticity.

- **Speak from your heart – not from a script, a teleprompter, or a speech that someone else wrote or prepared.** Sincerity in speaking, not reading, makes your message transferable.

I am throwing down the gauntlet. Get better as a public speaker.

IF YOU BREAK THE LAW: There will be an obvious lack of impact. You will be subject to minor interruptions by the prospect (more coffee, phone calls, and people walking in to get answers). The customer will be stoic, and you will be trying to judge him and figure out what his body language is saying. Let me help you understand: YOU'RE BORING!

IF YOU FOLLOW THE LAW: You'll see smiles. You'll see other people being called into the meeting. You'll see a willingness on the part of the customer to both listen and participate. You'll notice questions being asked that will positively impact their decision to buy. And you'll be having a great time, instead of trying to figure out body language and when to "close."

Not only will you get the order, there's also a reputation bonus. After the dynamic performance is over, the customer will talk about you proactively in a positive way.

CAUTION: This is not a one-time lesson. It's a lifetime lesson. Start now.

AHA! When you're making your presentation to a customer, it must be with passion and transferable belief.

The lost secret of evaluating your presentation skills: record yourself.

KEY TO IMPLEMENTATION: Record yourself weekly, and listen actively – which means: take notes. Judging your own performance is the fastest route to improvement. Enroll in a Dale Carnegie course. It will not just teach you, it will enable you and empower you beyond your self-imposed limits.

Sing karaoke. I know it sounds weird, but it will give you the understanding that words are sung, not just spoken. And it will give you insight into the performance aspect of communicating.

Own and read my *Little Green Book of Getting Your Way*. To convert your presentation to a performance takes time and a renewed amount of dedication (especially if you already think you're "pretty good").

Unbreakable Law

20

ATTRACT, ENGAGE, AND CONNECT SOCIALLY

CHALLENGE

Less than ten years ago, if you wanted to meet a prospect, it was all about live networking – showing up, talking, engaging, exchanging business cards, and trying to connect and get appointments with a few people. Now there's LinkedIn, and other social media outreaches that allow you to find more targeted people faster, and connect with them virtually.

REALITY: You cannot do one OR the other. In today's world, both online networking AND face-to-face networking must be mastered. My early networking in Charlotte, North Carolina, paved my way for local business success. My online networking has expanded my reputation and brand in a way I could never have imagined. You have the same opportunities. The unanswered question is: How are you taking advantage of them?

Business Cards May Be on the Way out. How Are You Connecting?

I'm in Las Vegas at The Venetian having coffee at Espressamente Illy where they serve (arguably) the world's best coffee. At the bar, I recognize someone obviously not from America. (Fashion reveals all.)

"Where are you from?" I asked. "Belgium," he replied triumphantly and with pride. "I'll buy your coffee," I said. "As a welcome to America."

He said, "I'm also buying coffee for two of my friends." I said, "Fine, put it on my bill!"

We began to exchange cultural information, and I discovered all three of them were in sales, like me. Their name badges revealed that they are attendees of the same conference I am a featured speaker at tomorrow evening.

Now we had a link.

They wanted to know what I knew, and I wanted to know what they knew.

Marcel's (one of the group) first question to me was one I have been asked a thousand times, "What's the secret of selling against fierce competition?" My immediate answer was, "Differentiate with value, or die with price."

He said, "I agree. I'm a value provider."

I said, "Hey, let's tweet it," and immediately we turned the conversation to social media. I asked them how many followers they had on twitter. The first guy had none. The second guy had none. The third guy, Marcel, said, "Not too many," and sheepishly smiled.

Turns out they wanted to use social media, but they just didn't know how to use it.

NOTE: I am amazed at how many savvy business people don't take the AHA! or impactful information shared or exchanged in a business conversation and send it out to the world.

IT'S YOUR CHOICE: You can tell three people, or 30,000 people – even 3,000,000 people. The power of Twitter, when applied to business social media, allows you to broadcast your brilliance to your followers and all the followers of those who re-tweet you. From a casual conversation in a coffee bar. WOW!

We spoke for an hour. We had lots to talk about. I gave them my business card, my business coin card, and two signed books and said, "May I have your business cards?" Each of them said, "I didn't bring any," and I thought to myself, that doesn't work.

But my thinking was 1990, not 2013.

REALITY: Pascal, the guy I bought the coffee for said, "Just connect with me on LinkedIn." Cool.

Business cards are not necessary to connect anymore, especially if they're boring, or have been created by some marketing department, or both.

Right then we each took out our mobile devices and connected with one another on LinkedIn. Not a business card, rather an online business connection – a permanent business card, a permanent connection. And with the exchange, we each receive 100 times more information than what could ever fit on a business card.

BUSINESS SOCIAL MEDIA LESSION LEARNED: When you link with people, like people, follow people, photo with people, "bump" with people, and tweet what is said, all of the sudden the business card becomes relatively irrelevant.

EPILOGUE: Less than an hour later, twenty-two global re-tweets of "Differentiate with value, or die with price." And the re-tweets are still piling up.

TRY THIS: Next time you attend a networking event, don't bring any business cards. Force people to link with you, or follow you, if they want to connect with you.

Realize that a business card only really represents a simple exchange, but that a LinkedIn or Twitter or Facebook on-the-spot connection creates engagement.

Long-term engagement.

Think about the pile of business cards on your desk from people that you've never really connected with, and certainly have never provided value for. Then think about the number of people who you could be adding to your network – people who could really be enlightened by you and discover your depth.

The tide is turning against one of America's institutions. It's not a "movement" or a "protest." Rather, it's a technological evolution. And one you and I need to be made aware of – today.

Oh, business cards will be here for some time, but I can already hear my three-year-old granddaughter, Isabel, asking me fifteen years from now, "Pop Pop, what's a business card?"

How are you connecting?

It's not just your business card. It's the perceived value of your connection.

JEFFREY GITOMER

Who's Afraid of Social Media and Social Networking? You Are!

You're a chicken. Let me correct that. You're a dumb chicken.

You're out in the middle of the road, pecking for scraps of food, and an eighteen-wheeler is about to run you over.

LET ME EXPLAIN: Business social media has created the biggest chicken farm in the history of mankind.

But you're too chicken to get involved with, or participate in, what has already proven to be the biggest boom to business and sales since the creation of the Internet.

The chicken farm is also known as "Corporate America."

Since a very small percentage of salespeople and business people in the country are taking total advantage of business social media, I'm assuming you fall into the chicken category. And I'm not just talking corporations and lawyers here. I'm saying you, the salesperson, are a chicken.

Here are the elements that may be holding you back from participating in Facebook, LinkedIn, Twitter, and YouTube to build your connections, your reputation, your business, and (of course) your sales:

1. You're technologically challenged. You may feel overwhelmed at the thought of creating your own business Facebook page, your own LinkedIn account, your own Twitter account, and certainly your own YouTube channel. RELAX. Each one of these social media programs has easy-to-follow tutorials that will allow you to get started and establish your base. It will require an investment of time, about two to three hours total. Or, in that same period of time, you could make twenty cold calls and receive twenty rejections. Think about it.

2. You don't know where to begin. Begin by calling your top twenty-five customers to find out what they consider valuable in their marketplace and in their business. Inform them you're about to create a value-based business social media presence and you'll be sending them an email asking them to join you.

3. You don't know which program to start with. Start with Facebook. Currently the third largest country in the world, Facebook has now interconnected more than a billion people, many of whom are your customers and your prospects. You may already have a personal Facebook account. Now start a Facebook "business" page.

4. You don't know what to say. When you call your customers and find out what they want to hear, what they want to read, and what they want to learn about, you'll know exactly what to say. Business social media is not complex. It's not a course in calculus or physics. The secret basically revolves around using common sense and providing value. Those are the core elements.

5. You don't understand how it applies to business. Business social media provides a first ever, open forum where customers can connect with you and share their feelings, and you have an opportunity to respond back. If you don't see how it applies to business, perhaps you should search your competitors, who are at this moment making some feeble attempt to get involved. Your job is to create a better, more open, more truthful forum on Facebook, on Twitter, and on YouTube.

6. You're afraid your customers will post something bad. Wake up and smell the Internet. Just because you don't give customers an opportunity to post bad news doesn't mean they're not going to post it. If you give them an opportunity to post, it will give you an opportunity to respond and fix the problem, or at least address it – thereby giving your other customers assurance that you're paying attention. This is also a huge opportunity for your business to discover your own weaknesses and make certain they don't reoccur. I believe a negative post on your business Facebook page is one of the most positive opportunities you could have. And the only people against it are C-level chickens and marketing chickens. Oh wait, I left out lawyer chickens.

7. You're afraid the boss will fire you. If you're posting positive comments about customer interactions and customers themselves are posting their comments about how much they love you, your fear of being fired could turn into a raise. Most of the time bosses are afraid of business social media because they are technologically challenged themselves.

NOTE WELL: All bosses and all sales managers are chickens. That's why they put a non-compete clause in your contract in the first place.

8. You're afraid you will break the rules arbitrarily set by your corporate attorneys. The easiest way to ensure that you stay away from rules is to stay away from your company name. Your business Facebook page should be about the product or the service, not the company. Keep in mind, you're branding yourself and you're branding your expertise. This is all about communicating and helping customers, not selling products.

9. You're afraid no one will follow you. If you set up a page and use the *Field of Dreams* strategy, "If you build it they will come," you are correct. No one will follow you. If you create a game plan as outlined above, post valuable information, and invite your customers to follow you, you'll have more followers than you can say grace over.

10. You're afraid to make the personal commitment. Time fears and time commitments are one of the biggest barriers of life, not just business social media. I recommend that you list the hours of a day that you're awake, maybe sixteen, maybe eighteen, whatever it is, and allocate them to the projects you consider most important, saving at least two hours for business social media. One hour in the morning and an hour in the evening.

NOTE WELL: If your boss is silly enough to forbid Facebook at work, start the morning at Starbucks. Make twenty-five connections, post five great events, and cruise into work an hour late. After a week, the boss will ask what you're up to. Show 'em. You might be able to get a rule changed.

10.5. Your bosses and lawyers are not just afraid of business social media, they're afraid of everything. Business paranoia is among the funniest and most pathetic aspects of free enterprise.

REALITY: Look at the companies that took the social media step first. They're the leaders. They talk to their customers, rather than hide from them. And the customers are becoming more loyal in the process.

HERE'S A HINT: Ask the company CEO and lawyer to tell you what you CAN do, not what you can't.

The simple answer to involvement and achieving business social media success is *seek professional help.* I did. One Social Media (onesocialmedia.com) advises me how to cross-link, keyword, and take other Googleable actions. It's working.

Reallocate time. Two hours a day to start. Get into the 21st century. It's measurable, and it's pleasurable.

IF YOU BREAK THE LAW: Breaking this law is more than obvious – it's costly. You're noticed as much by your absence as you are by your presence. Especially your strong presence. Social presence, both in person and virtual, is the driver of your reputation and your impact – both in business and as an individual.

Here are the business social media minimums. If you haven't reached them, you're breaking this law:

Facebook: 1,000+ "likes"

Twitter: 1,000+ followers

LinkedIn: 501+ connections

YouTube: 10 videos and 1,000 views

Blog: 500 RSS subscribers

Weekly E-zine: 500 subscribers

Face-to-Face Networking: 10 hours a week

Still think you haven't broken this law?

IF YOU FOLLOW THE LAW: When you attract, engage, and connect socially, people will be joining, linking, liking, re-tweeting, and posting positive stuff about you, your products, and your business.

Oh, and your phone will be ringing with people who want to buy. If you're looking to attract customers, following this law is the BEST way.

CAUTION: Whether you meet online or face-to-face, the other person is going to check your prowess and reputation when the meeting is over. And you can't stop them.

AHA! Social media can provide reputation, referrals, and sales.

AHA! Social media is the new cold call.

Social media interaction is one-on-one involvement with customers that the entire world can see.

AHA! Your individual participation in social media is not an option; it's an imperative.

AHA! The community where you live and work is just as important as your online community – especially when you're spending dollars locally.

KEY TO IMPLEMENTATION: FOLLOW ME! STUDY ME! COPY ME! I have set the example of how to get your social network going, AND I'm making my process easy to replicate.

- **Start tweeting value messages once a day. Send a few samples to your list and ask them to follow you by clicking a link.**
- **Get to 501 LinkedIn connections, and post your thoughts.**
- **Talk to customers on your business Facebook page. Encourage more posts by responding.**
- **Start a YouTube channel by using your smart phone as your camera and posting device. Create videos worth watching.**

Then GET OUT OF THE OFFICE and meet people. Before work, at lunch, and after work, networking opportunities abound. The easiest rule is "go where your customers go." Build relationships and meet new people who could become valuable connections.

Unbreakable Law

21

EARN WITHOUT ASKING

CHALLENGE

All salespeople want to *make* sales, *ask* for referrals, and *beg* for some letter of testimonial. Luckily, you're not like all salespeople. The key to sales success is the word "earn." You *never* have to close a sale if you earn it and you never have to ask for a referral if you earn it.

Seems simple on the surface, but "earning" is the hardest element of sales to master. It's not just a process, it's a game changer, and THE report card of your effort, your relationship, and your perceived value. And, oh yeah, your money.

Closing the Sale...the Definitive Answers You Won't Like.

What makes sales happen? Your words, your actions, your perceived differentiation, and your perceived value.

Not your ask!

What makes referrals happen? Your actions, your service, your WOW!

Not your ask!

"A - B - C. Always Be Closing."

You may know that line from the infamous sales movie, *Glengarry Glen Ross*, when Alec Baldwin plays himself. It's a throwback sales training line from the 1960s that manifested itself all the way to the '00s. The problem with that line is some people are still using it.

Whenever I do a seminar, everyone wants to know the *fastest* way to close the sale, the *easiest* way to close the sale, and the *best* way to close the sale.

REALITY: There is no fast way, there is no easy way, and there is no best way to close the sale. The fastest, easiest, and best way is to get the customer to BUY.

However, there is a better way than thinking of it as closing the sale. And once you understand what that way is, it will change your approach to the sale, for the better, forever...

It's not the "close," it's the open.

From the moment you engage the prospective customer, they're beginning to make a judgment. First they judge you, then they judge what they're buying, and finally they judge what company they're buying it from. As I've said for years, the first sale that's made is the salesperson (that would be you).

THE SECRET OF SELLING CAN BE DEFINED IN FOUR WORDS: Perceived value and perceived difference. Two of the four words are the same: perceived.

If your prospective customer perceives no difference between you and the competition, and perceives no value (better stated, a greater value) in what you're offering, then all that's left is price – and you will most likely lose the sale. Or, if you win the sale, it will be at the expense of your profit.

There are two intangibles that, when combined, create a better chance and a better percentage, of you completing the sale. They are "comfort" and "fit." How comfortable were you with the prospective customer? How comfortable was the prospective customer with you? And was there a perceived fit? Did what you were selling fit with what the customer needed or wanted to buy?

So I'm going back to my original statement: *It's not the close, it's the open.*

Let me give you a pop quiz that will help you determine whether or not you were even ready to open...

How is your attitude? How strong is your belief system? Do you have a GREAT attitude? Do you have an impenetrable belief in your company, your products or services, and yourself? Do you also believe that the customer is better off having purchased from you?

How well have you researched both the company and the person that you're meeting with? Preparation for the sale is broken down into three parts: personal preparation, sales preparation, and preparation in terms of the prospect – with this critical caveat: PREPARATION IN TERMS OF THE PROSPECT.

Do you know what their reasons for buying are? Do you know what their motive(s) for buying might be? If you know their reasons and their motives, by definition, you will also know their urgency.

NOTE WELL: Your reasons for selling pale in comparison to their reasons for buying.

When you first spoke on the phone with the prospect, was it a friendly encounter? Were you familiar with them? Were they familiar with you? Did you develop rapport? Do you have anything in common?

HERE'S THE SECRET: Prior to your face-to-face appointment or your telephone appointment to complete the sale, and in addition to your preparation, you must have a goal for the customer to like you, believe you, have confidence in you, and trust you. If those goals are not achieved within the framework of the sales presentation, then the completion of the sale will never become a reality.

Paraphrasing my opening statement: If it doesn't start right, it won't end right.

Rather than learning or regurgitating some time-worn "close," start yourself on the path to "earn" by asking yourself these questions at the end of every presentation:

- **How ready were you?**

- **How friendly were you?**

- **How emotionally engaging were you?**

- **How different were you?**

- **How valuable were you?**

- **How compelling were you?**

- **How believable were you?**

- **How credible were you?**

- **How self-confident were you?**

- **How relatable were you?**

- **How trustworthy were you perceived to be?**

These are hard questions. But the answers will automatically bring new awareness to your presentation, and the results, after a month or so of self-analysis, will open sales doors and fill your wallet.

Closing the sale is not an action. It's a culmination and a sum total of the elements that make a favorable decision possible.

The close of a sale is a delicate balance between your words and deeds and the prospect's thoughts and perceptions.

A sale is always made. Either you sell the prospect on yes, or they sell you on no.

- **It's not the responsibility of the salesperson to close the sale. It is the responsibility of the salesperson to engage the prospect.**

- **It's not the responsibility of the salesperson to close the sale. It is the responsibility of the salesperson to prove differentiation to the prospect.**

- **It's not the responsibility of the salesperson to close the sale. It is the responsibility of the salesperson to prove value to the prospect.**

- **It's not the responsibility of the salesperson to close the sale. It is the responsibility of the salesperson to earn the sale.**

Don't close the sale. Complete the sales process, *earn* the sale, and begin the relationship.

Earning the sale is all about the laws you've learned so far – your attitude, your ability to serve, your ability to prove, your total knowledge, your mastery of technology, your reputation, and your ability to express yourself in a positive, engaging way.

Free Git͡Bit...If you are interested in the eight personal barriers that you create before or during the sale, go to www.gitomer.com and enter the word BARRIER in the GitBit box.

You give me a prepared, friendly, engaging, different, valuable, compelling, believable, self-confident, relatable, trustworthy salesperson... and I'll give you a sale!

JEFFREY GITOMER

Earning Referrals Is Harder Than Earning Sales.

I'm angry about the (mis)information offered by "experts" about referrals.

I'm not angry that the majority of their information is totally off base and bogus, I'm angry you might believe it, take it to heart, try it, fail miserably, and lose both relationships and customers.

My anger centers around the word ASK.

Some idiot, *er, I mean expert,* said you MUST ask in order to receive your fair share. He babbled on to state there's a "Rule of 20-60-20." He claims that 20% of your customers will always give you a referral, 60% will give you a referral only if you ask them, and 20% will never give you one.

Where on earth did that rule come from?

HERE'S MY RULE: 20% of your customers *may* give you a referral if you ask; the other 80% are somewhere between uncomfortable and pissed.

Pareto (who in 1906 created the 80-20 Principle that was later redefined by Joseph Moses Juran in 1941) is turning over in his grave at people who make up statistics with ZERO basis in fact.

Your boss will tell you, "As soon as you make a sale, ask for a referral."

REALITY: There is no worse time to ask.

Or your boss will remind you, "Don't forget to ask for referrals." This is just as ridiculous.

If you're determined to ask, you better know WHEN to ask. Too early and you're dead. At least let the relationship blossom. At least let your product or service begin to evolve into a favorable outcome.

GENERAL RULES OF ASKING FOR A REFERRAL: If it feels awkward, DON'T ASK. If you don't have a solid relationship, DON'T ASK. If you ask for a referral and don't get one, DON'T ASK AGAIN.

MY RULE OF ASK: Don't ask. Earn.

There are 5.5 major consequences of asking for a referral:

1. **You create unnecessary tension in your relationship.**

2. **You may not have done anything to earn one yet.**

3. **You put your customer in an awkward position.**

4. **If you don't get one, consider it a report card, not a lack of response.**

5. **If you follow up with an email or a phone call "reminding" your customer you haven't received the referral you asked for, it could destroy the relationship.**

5.5 **If you call and ask, and they don't give you one, and you call and ask AGAIN, it's likely they'll never take your call again.**

INSIGHT: Way before referrals occur, you'd better understand what makes referrals happen. Your actions make referrals possible – or not.

Now that you understand why some people may be reluctant to refer you (especially if you ask, more especially if you ask too soon, most especially if you ask twice), let me give you the best strategy to get all kinds of referrals. It involves a one-word action plan: EARN!

- **Earn referrals with value perceived by the customer in the relationship.**

- **Earn referrals with value-based actions.**

- **Earn referrals with quality of relationship.**

- **Earn referrals with memorable service.**

- **Earn referrals with quality of product.**

- **Earn referrals with reliability.**

- **Earn referrals with consistency.**

- **Earn referrals with speed of response.**

NOTE WELL: It's not just one earning action that will open the referral floodgates. It's all of them. These are actions that build loyalty and reputation – and referrals are the result and the report card.

THE BIG SECRET: Give one.

BEST STRATEGY FOR GIVING A REFERRAL: Arrange a lunch meeting, and bring a referral for your customer. Your customer will be dumbfounded. He or she will be ever so grateful and will talk about you and the incident for years. Oh, by the way, your customer will go out of their way to provide you with TWO referrals as a genuine thank you.

CAUTION: This requires work beyond the sale on your part.

NOTE WELL: Even if your customer does not reciprocate, you're on the path to understanding Unbreakable Law 9: Deliver Value First.

Free Git ⋏Bit ...There's one more strategy for getting referrals. To get it, go to www.gitomer.com and enter the word REWARD in the GitBit box.

IF YOU BREAK THE LAW: By definition it means you have not earned. Asking for a referral is by far the riskiest aspect of building a relationship. Asking for a referral or a testimonial means it's too soon to have earned it. You put your customer into a SUPREME position of discomfort if he or she doesn't want to give one. And if there's anything worse than asking for a referral or testimonial, it's asking for one twice. I define asking twice as greed and stupidity – so does your customer.

IF YOU FOLLOW THE LAW: It means you have become a member of the elite group of sales professionals. Only the top 5% of salespeople in the world get this message. It means you have established real relationships with your customers and are reaping the rewards that go along with it.

- **Earning a sale means you have gained a measure of perceived value.**

- **Earning a referral means you have gained a measure of trust.**

- **Earning a testimonial means you have gained a measure of loyalty.**

- **Earning all three is the ultimate all-around win.**

CAUTION: Don't keep score. Just keep giving referrals. Even if the customer doesn't "pay you back," the world will pay you back times ten.

AHA! Every time you walk into a sales call, think OPEN and ENGAGE.

AHA! Asking for a sale means you're still competing. Asking for a sale means you're uncertain of outcome. And asking for a sale means a strong possibility of either no, not yet, or some form of stall.

AHA! The sale is made emotionally (perception), then justified logically (mentally).

AHA! I have used these two questions to help move customers to the contract: Are you ready? Is that fair enough?

The single most powerful sales lead is an unsolicited referral.

The second easiest way to gain referral: earn it. The easiest way to earn a referral: give one.

KEY TO IMPLEMENTATION: Study your last ten sales. Did you ask or earn? Record your sales presentation once a week. It will be the single most revealing, most realistic, and uncomfortable training of your life. It will also be the best lesson in who you are, and how you present.

Study your last ten referrals. Did you ask or earn? Go back to the people who referred you and ask them why they did it, and would they do it again.

The one-word definition of referral is RISK.

Your customer is willing to risk the relationship he or she has with someone and trust that you will respect it, honor it, and build it.

JEFFREY GITOMER

LOVE IT OR LEAVE IT

CHALLENGE

How much do you love your job? I mean really? Would you work for free? Do you admire your leaders? Do you have deep belief in your company and your products? Is your passion evident and transferable when you present to prospects? And finally, if you could sell anything, anyplace, is this where you would be?

These are the questions you have to ask yourself, because the answers will determine your future, your earnings, and your fate.

Are You Burned Out or Just Hating It?

I just read an article about someone's totally bogus opinion of "job burnout." It made me realize some people actually are (or think they are) "burned out."

A quick search on Amazon revealed 580 books that contain the title, or address the subject of "job burnout." Yikes!

The article I read proposed a remedy of "do less and you'll avoid burnout." It also recommended to avoid excessive workload, don't be overly accommodating, avoid people who drain your energy, do not overwork yourself, and they threw in job disillusionment.

IN OTHER WORDS: You'll still hate it, but you'll hate it less.

Why do people claim they're burned out?

It's a self-inflicted thought wound based on:

- **Taking inappropriate action**
- **The false feeling of being overwhelmed and stressed out**
- **Having a negative work atmosphere in general**
- **Not really loving your job**
- **Not believing in what you do**
- **Having a boss who is somewhere between a jackass and an idiot**

While burnout and stress are real, often they're self-imposed feelings that you can overcome.

Burnout manifests itself in your daily talk until it's embedded into your psyche. Not good.

You can begin your self-actualization by asking reality-based questions of yourself. Write down the answers.

QUESTION ONE: How much you love your job?

QUESTION TWO: What's the BEST part of your job?

QUESTION THREE: What would you rather be doing?

QUESTION FOUR: Where would you rather be working that could afford you the same or better opportunity (not just money)?

QUESTION FIVE: Is the grass really greener on the other side of employment?

Being or feeling burned-out or stressed-out is not a problem; it's a symptom. "Why" you feel you're burned out is the heart of the situation.

Once you ask yourself these questions, it's time to DO SOMETHING POSITIVE ABOUT IT.

Relief begins when you identify "cause," continues when you find your own answers and discover the truth (about you), and arrives when you realize you can change your thought pattern from burned out to ON FIRE!

ACTION ONE: Write down what you believe is causing the stressful feelings.

ACTION TWO: Write down what you believe the remedy could be.

ACTION THREE: Beside each remedy, write down what you or others could be doing.

ACTION FOUR: Write down the likelihood of these remedies occurring.

ACTION FIVE: Write down your ideal job or career, and then write down what you have to do or learn to get there.

DECIDE if you are in or out of your job. If in, rededicate yourself to personal excellence. If out, get out quick.

REALITY: Based on your present situation (family, debt, obligations) you may just have to endure it for a while. But if you have identified causes and remedies, calm begins to occur. You have it under control. You're making decisions.

Your present circumstance has to be measured against your present situation and future hopes and dreams.

Here are a few suggestions for what will take you from "burnout" mode into a more positive and hopeful frame of mind:

1. **Start your day with the three most important things you want to accomplish.**

2. **Cancel all stupid and time-wasting meetings.**

3. **Stop talking about things that don't matter, especially other people.**

4. **Focus on outcome, not just task.**

5. **Dedicate at least fifteen minutes a day to thinking by yourself.**

6. **Get rid of three major time wasters (attention diverters):**
   - **Facebook notifications at work (unless it's business Facebook)**
   - **Personal emails and personal calls**
   - **Negative water fountain chit chat**

7. **Go home from work and read instead of watch. Start with my *Little Gold Book of YES! Attitude.***

7.5 **Review your accomplishments at the end of each day – to both praise yourself and challenge yourself. Write them down.**

Restart your personal fire. Give yourself a chance to become BEST at your job and your career. Never give in to self-defeat. Decide every day that you can only be your best by doing your best.

Become BEST, not burnt.

Which Way Do I Go to Find Success?

I get at least one email a day telling me I can be a success if I just pay the sender a bunch of money and do it their way. The reason these people succeed with "do it my way" ideas is that most unsuccessful people don't have the confidence to do it on their own. They have no game plan and figure, "Well, if that guy did it, maybe I can too."

The people who "pay for success" begin to reach for money based on *greed*, rather than earning money based on drive or love. More often than not, they fail at the process and blame the guy that sold them the formula (or the formula itself).

When you reach for success and can't quite get there, see it as a lesson and an adventure – not a failure. And if you consider it a failed attempt, take a look at your attitude *first*.

At no charge to you, here's my 4.5-step formula for success:

1. **Find something to do that you believe in and that you love.**

2. **Dedicate the time that it takes to become a world-class expert at it.**
   (NOTE: I was taught long ago there are three kinds of experts. An expert, a world-class expert, and THE world-class expert. In order to get where you want to go, in order to become successful, you have to be at least a world-class expert.)

3. **You have to believe in yourself and let no one else shake that belief.**

4. **You have to wake up every morning with an attitude of YES! and have it be strong enough to shake off the NOs.**

And, if you have all of those elements...

4.5 **You must then be willing to work hard. Not just "do whatever it takes," but actually see the vision of completion and fulfillment, and work hard toward that with all your heart, every day.**

SUCCESS FORMULA RECAP: If you love it, if you believe in it, if you believe in yourself, and if you're willing to work your butt off, you can march to success doing it YOUR way.

I just gave you the formula. But why aren't you moving on it? Why aren't you jumping at it?

I'll tell you why:

- **I haven't told you the story about how I came upon this theory.**
- **I haven't shown you any proof that my way works.**
- **You want more "how" details.**
- **You have no idea what you want to do.**
- **You have no idea what you would love to do.**
- **You are unwilling to take the risk (a form of low belief).**
- **You are unwilling to chance not having rent or car payment money.**
- **You don't really want it that bad.**

Most people have little or no real passion for what they do every day. They're dreaming about achieving success in other ways than the opportunity at their feet. (Maybe it's time to read or re-read *Acres of Diamonds*, by Russell Conwell.)

Your success will not be achieved with someone else's formula UNLESS the product or service they're involved with matches your passion.

The success formula your looking for is within you. All you have to do to find it is arrange some personal alone time to think about it and discover it. It may involve shutting off the TV for a while and giving yourself mental freedom to read or write.

Once you have the idea, you have to make a plan. Not just a plan to execute – a plan to clarify your thinking and smooth out the details before you leap into action – full force (the only way to take action).

THERE'S ONE MORE ELEMENT: Courage. You've gotta have the guts and fortitude to start, continue, stay the course, make it happen, and celebrate the victory.

You create the idea, you create the plan, you make the map, you develop the passion, you take the first step, and you march to success.

You have known of the lessons since the first time you watched Dorothy in *The Wizard of Oz*. If you have brains, heart, courage, and the unyielding desire to get to Oz, success can be yours.

You don't need to be a wizard. Just be you.

IF YOU BREAK THE LAW: This law is unbreakable because failure to love what you do creates a void in your character and your growth. Lack of loving what you do compromises your ideals, your beliefs, your attitude, your drive, and your ability to create a passionate, transferable message. Lack of love of what you do also affects your concentration, dedication, and focus. Oh, it will also compromise your income. You won't love that either.

IF YOU FOLLOW THE LAW: You'll be doing things naturally. Your belief and passion will be transferable. So will your message. You'll be following and living the immortal theme from Dale Carnegie's classic books, *How to Win Friends and Influence People* and *How to Stop Worrying and Start Living: Be Yourself!* When you offer your true self, it leads to truthful dialogue. Truth becomes the basis of trust and relationship. And when you love what you do, what you represent, and who you represent, the customer will BUY, become loyal, and refer others.

CAUTION: Please don't tell me "you need the job," if you don't love it. Or "this is just temporary," if it's not your passion. I'm not buying it. Those phrases indicate you're willing to "settle" and lack the courage to risk. Sadly, many will settle for a lifetime of mediocrity and regret, even bitterness or cynicism, never knowing what could have been.

BIGGER CAUTION: Don't quit your day job too soon. Make a plan. Have a capital (money) cushion. Make a safe exit. Don't burn a bridge or leave a trail.

BIGGEST CAUTION: When you get what you want, you'd better be ready. If you're planning on leaving soon, you'd better be studying now. Arrive prepared.

AHA! Ask yourself: "Would I do this for free?" (If it helps you gain experience at what you really want to do, then I recommend working someplace for free, but set limits of both time and a hard end date.)

AHA! Ask yourself: "Is this job moving me forward?" "What would I rather be doing?" "Do I have the courage to take the step toward fulfillment?"

KEY TO IMPLEMENTATION: Loving your job, loving your product, loving your company, and loving your life, will double your sales. MAJOR HELP: Read *The Outliers*, by Malcolm Gladwell. It will help you understand how dedication to doing what you love will bring you good fortune, give you good fortune, and earn you a fortune. Don't make a game plan. Make a life plan. Define your perfect career, job, and place to perform it. Now compare it to what you're doing. Ouch. Create a map that will get you from "here" to "there." Convert the energy of "fear of failing" to "excitement for adventure and success." FLY!

If you love what you do, your passion will lead you to success, and your success will lead to your fulfillment.

JEFFREY GITOMER

Take the Right Action.

There is ONE LAW that stands way above all the other laws. It stands so high that it's above being a "number." Actually it's part of all the other laws, and it's what makes all the other laws happen. It is: take the right action.

I could have said *take action*. But that doesn't guarantee you'll take the RIGHT action. Actions that will help you master the law, earn your reputation, make more sales, and build your brand, your relationships, and customer loyalty leading to repeat business and referrals.

I think you get the picture.

REALITY: Each law can only be mastered by taking the right actions. And you are the (only) one responsible for taking them.

Here are the elements of taking the right actions:

TAKE THE RIGHT ACTION IN SPITE OF PRESSURE. Competition and compensation often drive short-term actions that will hurt you later.

TAKE THE RIGHT ACTION IN SPITE OF YOUR SALES PLAN. Not forcing the sale or making a self-serving recommendation. Rather, doing what's best for the customer.

TAKE THE RIGHT ACTION THAT IS IN YOUR CUSTOMER'S BEST INTEREST. For their productivity and profit, not your sales quota.

TAKE THE RIGHT ACTIONS FOR BOTH SHORT-TERM AND LONG-TERM SUCCESS. Make certain your short-term actions will stand the test of time.

TAKE ACTIONS THAT ARE IN HARMONY WITH YOUR CAREER GROWTH. Ethics and reputation are dictated by your actions.

TAKE ACTIONS IN YOUR FAMILY'S BEST INTEREST. Family first is your best strategy. They are the people that will always be there for you if the actions you take are always best for them.

Those are the actions – the right actions – that will lead to faster, easier, bigger sales now and forever.

Here are a few examples of taking action versus taking the RIGHT action:

- Taking action might mean making a follow-up call. Taking the RIGHT ACTION means that you have left the value message, or given the prospective customer information that helps them, not just asks for money.

- Taking action might mean carving out time to build relationships. Taking the RIGHT ACTION means you have made a daily appointment to meet with the customer and bring a prospective customer for them.

- Taking action might mean staying in touch with your customers on a weekly basis. Taking the RIGHT ACTION means you have sent your customer an email or an email magazine telling them how they can produce more, have better morale, be more profitable, or share a best practice.

THERE ARE TWO MORE FACTORS: They are the key to the "taking the right action" process. On the surface they seem conquerable, but let me assure you (based on fifty years of trying), they are the most challenging. They are *self-discipline* and *consistency.*

Your self-discipline is the driver of your consistency.

You want to lose weight, but you don't have the self-discipline or the consistency of taking the right actions to make it happen. You KNOW what to do and you know it's the RIGHT THING to do. Yet you don't do it.

You want to make more sales, but you don't have the self-discipline or the consistency of taking the right actions to make more sales happen. You KNOW what to do and you know it's the RIGHT THING to do. Yet you don't do it.

You substitute consistency for complacency. Not good.

HERE'S THE SECRET: Start small. Do the small things daily. Morning coffee with customers, weekly value messages to your email list, deciding on ONE THING AT A TIME and mastering that before you take on the next.

I have learned the value of self-discipline and consistency – both in fulfillment and monetary reward. This book is a classic example of my self-discipline AND my consistency. Writing is a self-discipline – writing twelve books is consistency.

All I need to do now is lose the weight.

You Must. I Need To. I Will.

Each of the 21.5 Unbreakable Laws of Selling was written as an actionable expression that you need to understand and apply in a way that makes your sales easier, faster, and bigger. This is the book's promise. And it's my promise. But *you* are the action taker and the mastery maker.

All of the laws are foundational to your sales success and have an immediate action you can take. For me, thinking of the laws as actions was the clearest path to the transferability of the book's message and promise. For you, it's a challenge to implement and master.

6.5 MINUTES THAT WILL CHANGE YOUR LIFE:

1. Go back to the table of contents and spend two minutes reading each law ALOUD, but put the words YOU MUST in front of each law as you read. The laws were designed to be commandments, or commands. Saying "you must" will create your understanding of the law.

2. Then spend another two minutes reading each law ALOUD, but this time put the words I NEED TO in front of each law as you read. This action will confirm your need to understand and desire to implement. Saying "I need to" will create your urgency to take action.

3. Then spend ANOTHER two minutes reading each law ALOUD, but put the words I WILL in front of each law as you read. Saying "I will" creates your affirmation and intention to master the law. Pretty cool, huh?

3.5 Then spend thirty seconds and select the five laws you believe will have the most impact on your success. Those can be the first laws you intend to master. (You can do it with a highlighter).

With this book, these laws, and your actions, you can build a brick and mortar foundation for your sales career and your personal success.

I hope you do!

Lather, Rinse, Repeat. Forever.

This book is not a one-time read. It's a lifetime read.

And now is the perfect time to make a plan, dedicate the time, set your intentions, and begin to take action toward mastery of EACH law.

MAJOR AHA! The 21.5 Unbreakable Laws of Selling are not just to be read. They're to be understood, put into action, and mastered. And in between reading and mastery, there's work. I'm calling it "money work." That way it seems more pleasurable. Certainly more doable.

And I'm going to make it as easy as pie.

I'm sure you will agree with me, this is a great book. And I'm certain you're saying to yourself, "I'm going to read this again."

I hope you do. But there's more. Much more. Mastering these laws are the FOUNDATION and KEY to your sales success and your career success. Only once more?

Don't just read it once more – Take the Unbreakable Laws online course and repeat it until you master it, forever.

I've spent my entire career as a writer documenting, describing, strategizing, and teaching every aspect of sales, loyalty, attitude, networking, trust, speaking, and leading.

This is my twelfth book and it will not be my last.

Ten more are on the drawing board.

HERE'S THE GREAT NEWS: All of my writings, books, and webinars are now available online. You can subscribe to "all Jeffrey, all the time" to view on demand from any device.

All you have to do is call me, or speak with any one of the friendly, helpful, intelligent people at my office.

OFFICE: 704.333.1112.
Our office hours are 24.7.365

At Lighthouse Beach,
Looking at My Reflection
in a Different Way.

How do you define the word "reflection?"

At the moment I'm outside on a sunny day overlooking the Pacific Ocean on the Oregon coast. The venue is called Lighthouse Beach because the Cape Arago Lighthouse is the prime visual attraction. Or is it?

Actually, the ocean waves are pounding against the beach and the rocks, creating majestic waterspray vistas that are indescribable. You gotta be here. You gotta see it.

I spent my first ten minutes in awe of the sight.

After that, I began to gather thoughts. Thoughts of other beautiful places I've been. Thoughts of undone things I gotta do. Dreams and intentions. And of course, just reveling in the moment.

As a writer this would be termed a "fantasy venue." As a thinker there could be no better place to conjure up all sorts of new thoughts.

REALITY: In the big picture of things, I am one grain of sand in the beach of life. Yet I'm here today basking in its glory. I'm grateful.

The ocean's relentless waves roll in whether I am here are not. Today is a rather calm day, but I've seen the ocean so violent here that it defies description. The wind, rain, and waves crash against the rocks – almost like the ocean is a cauldron with a one-million-degree fire.

"So what?" you're probably thinking. "You're on the beach watching the waves, and I'm here in my office working my ass off, or making cold calls, or out here sweating on a sales appointment, or following up with some guy who won't return my call, or (worse) being beaten by price."

Those are your issues, but in the heat of your mess, we do have something in common. *It's time for reflection.* Not the one you see in the mirror in the morning. I'm talking about a way bigger reflection than that. It's a reflection about time, accomplishment, achievement, and fulfillment. Life reflection.

When I was cold calling in New York City, often making sales, but more often getting my head handed to me, waves crashing on the beach never entered my mind. I was caught in the spiral of the process, failing to reflect on it and see what else could've been done, or how much smarter I could have (should have) been – how many more chances I should have taken.

What do you reflect on right now? And how are those reflections impacting your actions? Your achievements? Your success? Reflections are not just about sales – they're an important part of life. Your life.

Beyond sales, reflections are about people and moments and books that have impacted you. The lessons you have learned along the way. Things completed and things left undone. Your bucket list and the next thing to cross off. And your present situation and how you got there.

While it's a little easier for me to reflect right now, at some point in your life reflection will begin as well. I don't know the day, and neither do you. But I promise you it will happen. And when it does, it will mark the beginning of a new era – a big-picture era that no longer focuses on quota. Rather, it allows you to take a hard look at life. When that transition begins to happen your sales will double.

You'll no longer be fretting about the subject line in an email. Instead, you'll be taking actions to build your personal reputation, your personal brand, and your stature in your marketplace.

The transition will help you evolve from salesperson to sales leader. Not manager – leader. You lead your own charge, you lead your own way, and you lead your own plan to build your own reputation through the leadership you create with customers.

You are in charge of: The way customers speak about you. The way customers refer to you. The way customers refer other people to you. The way that customers reward you, not just with sales, but with referrals and accolades.

Hopefully those accolades will show up in your social media profiles or on their blog or their website, and most certainly on Google.

For some of you right now this makes no sense. Reason? Simple, you haven't begun the reflection process. Mark this page. Your day will come. And as I've said many times before, *when you get what you want you better be ready.*

Today I have clarity – ultimate clarity and understanding of what it took to make my sales (the reflection), and what it will take for you to increase your sales to a point where you can begin to reflect and bask in your own sunlight, at your own ocean, with your own waves pounding against the shore.

Pick a time, pick a place, and go.

EPILOGUE: During my coastal visit, I wrote much of the *21.5 Unbreakable Laws of Selling.* The Pacific Ocean's inspiration I felt while writing impacted those words. This book will help hundreds of thousands of salespeople (maybe more) build a solid sales foundation, better understand sales, execute their sales process in a more successful way, and make more sales to more people NOW!

Jeffrey Gitomer
Chief Executive Salesman

AUTHOR. Jeffrey is the author of *The New York Times* bestsellers: *The Sales Bible, Little Red Book of Selling, Little Black Book of Connections,* and *Little Gold Book of YES! Attitude.* All of his books have been number-one bestsellers on Amazon.com, including *Customer Satisfaction Is Worthless, Customer Loyalty Is Priceless*; *Little Red Book of Sales Answers, Little Green Book of Getting Your Way, Little Platinum Book of Cha-Ching!; Little Teal Book of Trust, Social BOOM!* and *Little Book of Leadership.* Jeffrey's books have sold millions of copies worldwide.

MORE THAN 100 PRESENTATIONS A YEAR. Jeffrey gives public and corporate seminars, runs annual sales meetings, and conducts live and Internet training programs on selling, YES! Attitude, trust, customer loyalty, and personal development. Jeffrey has also created a team of Gitomer Certified Speakers to bring his content to more audiences.

BIG CORPORATE CUSTOMERS. Jeffrey's customers include Coca-Cola, US Foodservice, Caterpillar, BMW, Verizon, MacGregor Golf, Hilton, Enterprise Rent-A-Car, AmeriPride, NCR, IBM, Comcast Cable, Time Warner, Liberty Mutual, Principal Financial, Wells Fargo Bank, BlueCross BlueShield, Carlsberg, Mutual of Omaha, AC Neilsen, Northwestern Mutual, MetLife, Sports Authority, GlaxoSmithKline, *The New York Post,* and hundreds of others.

IN FRONT OF MILLIONS OF READERS EVERY WEEK. Jeffrey's syndicated column, *Sales Moves,* appears in scores of business papers in the US and Europe, and is read by more than four million people every week.

ON THE INTERNET. Jeffrey's WOW website, www.gitomer.com, gets thousands of hits per week from readers and seminar attendees. His state-of-the-art presence on the web and e-commerce ability has set the standard among his peers and has won huge praise and acceptance from customers.

ONLINE SALES TRAINING. Jeffrey offers a wide variety of award-winning online sales training lessons. The content is pure Jeffrey – fun, pragmatic, real world – and can be immediately implemented. These individualized modules are leading the way in the field of customized e-learning.

LIVE WEBINARS. Jeffrey teams up with Ace of Sales CEO Andy Horner to present a series of cutting-edge webinars attended by thousands of businesspeople seeking to hone their selling, branding, relationship, communication, marketing, and success skills. Each webinar is meticulously crafted to be a training, entertaining, and inspirational experience filled with ideas, visuals, and techniques you can apply immediately.

SALES CAFFEINE. Jeffrey's weekly email magazine, *Sales Caffeine*, is a sales wake-up call delivered every Tuesday morning to more than 250,000 subscribers worldwide, free of charge. *Sales Caffeine* allows Jeffrey to communicate valuable sales information, strategies, and answers to sales professionals on a timely basis. To sign up, or for more information, visit www.salescaffeine.com.

BUSINESS SOCIAL MEDIA. Keep up with Jeffrey and his social media presence on Facebook, Twitter, LinkedIn, YouTube, and salesblog.com. New ideas, events, and special offers are posted daily. With more than 50,000 social media followers, and more than one million YouTube views, Jeffrey has built a groundswell of attraction and engagement.

SALES ASSESSMENT ONLINE. The world's first customized sales assessment, renamed a "successment," will judge your selling skill level in twelve critical areas of sales knowledge and give you a diagnostic report that includes thirty-six mini sales lessons. This amazing tool rates your sales abilities and explains your customized opportunities for sales growth.

ACE OF SALES. Jeffrey helped create the first customer relationship management (CRM) program that actually helps salespeople MAKE SALES, and it now has thousands of users. This incredible program must be previewed to be believed. To learn more and subscribe for a free trial, go to www.aceofsales.com.

SPEAKER HALL OF FAME. In 2008, Jeffrey was elected by his peers to the National Speaker Association's Speaker Hall of Fame. The designation, CPAE (Counsel of Peers Award for Excellence), honors professional speakers who have reached the top echelon of performance excellence. Inductees are evaluated by their peers through a rigorous and demanding process. Each candidate must excel in several categories: material, style, experience, delivery, image, professionalism, and communication.

Other Titles by Jeffrey Gitomer

LITTLE BOOK OF LEADERSHIP
(Wiley, 2011)

SOCIAL BOOM
(FT Press, 2011)

LITTLE TEAL BOOK OF TRUST
(FT Press, 2008)

THE SALES BIBLE, NEW EDITION
(HarperCollins, 2008)

LITTLE PLATINUM BOOK OF CHA-CHING!
(FT Press, 2007)

LITTLE GREEN BOOK OF GETTING YOUR WAY
(FT Press, 2007)

LITTLE GOLD BOOK OF YES! ATTITUDE
(FT Press, 2007)

LITTLE BLACK BOOK OF CONNECTIONS
(Bard Press, 2006)

LITTLE RED BOOK OF SALES ANSWERS
(FT Press, 2006)

LITTLE RED BOOK OF SELLING
(Bard Press, 2004)

CUSTOMER SATISFACTION IS WORTHLESS,
CUSTOMER LOYALTY IS PRICELESS
(Bard Press, 1998)

After you read each law, take the right action within the hour.

Reading followed by doing leads to mastery.

JEFFREY GITOMER